Tales And Prayers For New Life In Christ

Multiple-Use Life-Enriching Stories

Karl Evans

CSS Publishing Company, Inc., Lima, Ohio

TALES AND PRAYERS FOR NEW LIFE IN CHRIST

Copyright © 2008 by
CSS Publishing Company, Inc.
Lima, Ohio

Scripture quotations are from the Revised Standard Version of the Bible, copyrighted 1946, 1952 ©, 1971, 1973, by the Division of Christian Education of the National Council of the Churches of Christ in the USA. Used by permission.

Scripture quotations marked (NRSV) are from the New Revised Standard Version of the Bible, copyright 1989 by the Division of Christian Education of the National Council of the Churches of Christ in the USA. Used by permission.

Library of Congress Cataloging-in-Publication Data

Evans, Karl.
  Tales and prayers for new life in Christ : multiple-use life-enriching stories / Karl Evans.
    p. cm.
  ISBN 0-7880-2557-0 (perfect bound : alk. paper)
  1. Christian life. I. Title.

  BV4515.3.E93 2008
  242—dc22

                                                                              2007044340

For more information about CSS Publishing Company resources, visit our website at www.csspub.com or email us at csr@csspub.com or call (800) 241-4056.

Cover design by Barbara Spencer
ISBN-13: 978-0-7880-2557-0
ISBN-10: 0-7880-2557-0   PRINTED IN USA

This book is dedicated to all those lovely folks who have taught me the real validity, meaning, and value of telling stories as part of Christ's ministry. I thank my family for tolerating my stories. The congregations Donella and I have served have been occasionally puzzled by the process. The communities that have been our homes have been most supportive. The great books I have read have filled me with ideas. My teachers have occasionally been frustrated by my unbelief in their systems. Fellow students have prodded my vulnerable spots. Many others have just made it their life's mission to tell me more stories. All have made my life work much more fulfilling and my relationship with Christ much more precious.

Thanks to all of you for your help.

Karl Evans

Table Of Contents

Prologue   7

Why We Tell Jesus' Stories   11

What Do We Get From Stories?   14

The Revised Common Lectionary   17

An Open Book   19

Response To An Inspirational Story   20

New Hope United Methodist Church   25

Angie   28

Serving From The Bell Tower Is Not Easy   35

The Gentle Circle Of Aidan   38

Bishop Andrew — The Bishop's Sacrifice   43

Too Much Air   50

Bullpen Mud   52

What Is It To Be Human?   60

I Am Alone   63

The Innkeeper   64

Kava   67

Kick The Can   71

She's Still There	74
Lonny	78
Martin's People	85
Of Bread And Wine	91
The Flag On My House	95
One Fine Christmas Day	99
Pete	101
A Polish Christmas Carol	105
A Little Pushin' And Shovin'	112
A Vision Of Peace	118
Thank God For School!	120
The Starfish	122
The Strangest Dream	135
The Ladder	138
Ducks, Frogs, And Mud	144
The Big Feed	158

Prologue

Whoa! Whoever heard of a fight between a sidehill gouger and a wampus cat? Civilian Conservation Corps men and women, that's who. Such accounts enlivened the dreary hours of the CCC nights as long as the program continued to operate. This book is not about CCC life. It is, however, about the most boring hours many Christians suffer. Some hours of congregational life are as boring as CCC evenings. This is not necessary.

On the other hand, storytelling may be the most exciting life event open to every age group. This book intends to combine storytelling and congregational life in many ways. Our audience includes those who are cranky, happy, bored, tired, confused, or in any other condition known to humankind. I hope some will find themselves drawn to stories to embellish their own lives.

Whether times are tough or bountiful, stories help events string together as life experiences. Great valid stories are meaningful and valuable as life-development tools. This makes storytelling natural for Christian worship. Worship should be the most exciting part of any person's week. Therefore, this book is intended to be a source book for corporate congregational life, including worship.

Good stories are always part of strong community life. In about 1940, irrigation water came to the Black Canyon Irrigation District in Idaho. My parents chose to purchase some farmland between Fruitland and Parma. The residents of the area called the virgin community "Nu Acres." Water for farming made everything new. The land was virgin soil. Only God had ever plowed the land since creation. The land had never been plowed except by glacier. God covered the land with sagebrush, grass, and rabbit burrows. The first eighteen years of my life were spent on that land. My personal story involves family and community life in Nu Acres. We built our stories as we built up our homes and land.

The Bible is a book of similar stories. It is the book of building up the community that lies between Egypt, Turkey, and Iraq. Even today, we must include the Bible when we look for answers to the puzzles of Israel, Jordan, and Syria. We must also look to the Koran, the Enuma Elish, Ugarit documents, and so many others for illumination. Each has a story of its people to tell, and each is important in its own way.

These stories are not dead pages. These stories still live. They spread the word of the Creator in public meetings, private discussions, meditation, and in religious activities. Just as the Bible is critical to us, we must recall and tell our own stories in our own religious rituals and meditation. This is a simple task, but we need to write our own stories if they have value in our churches, synagogues, and temples. Church law does not usually require any congregation to use only biblical quotes in our worship. The sources must only be centered on the life of Christ. This book is a means to record some good stories, put them into usable format, and open them for congregational use.

In Nu Acres, Idaho, we were not alone building and strengthening the neighborhood. As years went along, the community slowly evolved. The Federal Bureau of Reclamation finally delivered irrigation water to the area. More families took the homestead leap and moved in.

We lived initially in tents, buses, shanties, or tar-paper shacks. Each family brought a new package of stories and relationships and issues with them. Each family had to clear its own sagebrush and build its own house and barn.

More to the point, each family sent its children to school. They took the family stories with them to the classroom. Every child went to the public school at some time. At the school, the children revealed something of their heritage.

Each family went to its choice of churches, Grange #428, and 4-H clubs. Everyone told the family secrets. Slowly we built our community.

While living with all this, life changed from inner-directed to outer-directed. The stories of the people shaped lives in wonderful ways. We did not really recognize the power of the change at the time. Those stories now make my heart pound as I listen to them again. If only I could remember more of them!

They were great stories. Ray Edmunson tells of hearing a young Eddie Arnold sing. Arnold began his music career as a small boy in

8

a community church in Tennessee. Ray and his new bride held hands while Arnold sang the stories of Jesus.

Sam Henne let sadness creep over his face as he talked of his own life. If pressed, he told of his youth as a Jew in Hitler's Germany. He eventually brought his young wife to America. They escaped Hitler together.

Slim Chesney was happy about losing only a hand in battle while in France. Others lost their lives. Even with only one hand, Slim was terrific with his team. Holes in the reins held securely onto the hook that replaced his arm. He then was free to tell fish stories and roll cigarettes with his only hand.

Another neighbor told of the horrors he experienced on the Bataan Death March. The Filipino people tried to sneak food to the American ghost soldiers along the route. His love and respect for those people have been part of me to this day.

Other stories added to the good feelings of the community — mostly. The neighbor whose cow stepped on his foot and broke it was a local hero and clown. The poor fellow stood on his broken foot in order to kick the cow with the other foot as punishment. He broke that foot, too. My friend tried to convince us he could not see the humor in his misfortune.

Another neighbor, in his late teens, was helping stack hay. His audience included several cute girls. He stuck his pitchfork completely through his foot. Oops!

Stories entertained the Grange #428 members, including me. Stories educated 4-H children, including me. Community tales helped in school, in church, or at family dinners. Stories made politics and romance live in our hearts. We were too young to directly experience them.

These stories defined the underlying truth and fabric of the community. We would not have been who we were apart from the existence of these stories. I have recorded some of those stories here.

I began to look for other stories that were having an impact on my life. This massive volume of tales, together, shaped me in so many ways. They were very close to me.

Key to our family life was our faith. We read the Bible a lot. Each of us had our own Bible. When we grew old enough to pretend we were reading, we expected to be given our own King James Version. The Bible my grandparents gave to me is still part of my library.

A clear sense of the nature of this great book lived in my mind's eye. I often sat quietly at the table at a family dinner — believe it or not! My ears feasted on the good tales from God. Soon I could read the Bible for myself.

I had the sense of God telling the sacred stories that shaped my existence. David, Moses, and Ruth were the principals of many, many of these wonderful stories. Words illuminating these heroes defined my family and me. They also defined my relationship with my God and with Jesus.

I would greatly enjoy buying a morning cup of coffee for Jesus any day. Jesus clearly has a special understanding of events of the world. He knows far more than I. Could I pick his brain on a few things? Would I? You bet I would!

On Christmas Eve, ten of us sat around the Christmas tree. We soaked in the stories of the stable and the angels. It was all so exciting! The stories told us we could become more than we had ever hoped to be.

On Easter morning the story mood changed as I milked the cows. I saw myself reliving that time in the minds and hearts of the women and disciples. Coming to the empty tomb had to be a wild experience. Easter changes everything for those who hear the story. This is the key to the use of the lectionary for corporate worship.

The Bible, community stories, and wild night parties made Nu Acres what it was for us. The community has now changed to reflect the realities of the current world. I left many years ago. Nu Acres will never be the same again. It will only change repeatedly.

Why We Tell Jesus' Stories

These stories were far more than just historical or fictional narratives. The words were not fictional fairy tales. They were the core events of human history in our little community.

The parables of Jesus had a unique and dominant role. Parables are simple translations of the unfathomable word of God into human language. Jesus uses them to describe the sacred vision for our lives. He also used them to invite us into that new world. It is the invitation into the new age that is most mysterious to us.

When the shepherd searched for the lost sheep, I was there. It was clear that God was inviting me to watch and wait for the call. I was a little impatient.

The mystery of the parable was a personal invitation to me. It seemed God wanted me to enter the task of finding and rescuing the sheep. That cloud of not knowing was a clear call to ministry. However, I tried to hide behind the mystery to avoid the call.

The parable of the ten young women at the wedding gave me a more basic challenge. I had to search my own life. I had to discover whether I was prepared to work for the kingdom. The mystery of the parable is the invitation to me to come into the kingdom. Why me? Why not me? Every parable has its own invitation to each person.

Following the face-to-face encounter with Jesus, the reality of the new world came forward. Meeting Jesus changed Paul and Silas and Peter and all the others. Their stories of meeting Christ moved me through the years following the cross and the tomb. They are mysteries, yet they are clear invitations into the new reality of the kingdom of Jesus.

Parables are often unique and wonderful stories of events yet to come. They give us hope for our world. These events exist now only in the vision of Christ. At the end of time, they will occur and enlighten us. They will be upon us like a thief in the night, but they will come.

The book of Revelation tells the vision of the world yet to come. The shape of society in the future is a wonderful mystery and story.

It is too wonderful to be left to chance. Those who know must tell the story.

With all this in mind, the internet and bookmobile question comes among us. How do we spread these stories around our world? How do we make them heard and witnessed by all the peoples of the earth? How can we ensure they will have their sacred effect?

Part of the answer, at least, is plain. The congregation. The people who have heard the stories must carry the weight of spreading them. We who have had changes made in us by these tales must repeat the stories.

One chief time of spreading these stories around is our corporate worship experience. Church gatherings on Sunday morning, evening, or midweek are like books in the human library. The stories they tell touch many lives and hearts.

In our worship, we work out our relationships with God and with each other. That is the task of worship. With only one God to recognize and respond to, our own possible actions seem limited.

We must respond to that one God in ways we consider best. God acts; we respond in our own manner. God rescues us from the burning desert; we respond by entering Jericho deeply committed. Perhaps God allows us to enter Babylonian captivity; we respond by whining about our bad luck. God comes as the Christ; we respond by turning away from the Christ or by turning toward him.

In all of this, one thing is certain. God will act in our best interests. That is the definition of love, and God is love. Our only choice is in how we will respond to God's activity in our lives. The stories become the actions, descriptions, and guidelines for God's actions and our responses. The stories become the foundation for our community.

This is the work of worship. The stories of God's action and our response has become the core of worship. These stories are the core elements of our faith development. They build our faith. Whether laid out for us as responses, narratives, prayers, songs, or blessings, these stories change us somehow. Regardless of our personal intent, they build our relationships with each other and with God. That is why we tell stories in worship.

The stories within this book have served in many, many different ways. No story has only one format allowed to it. Some make prayers. Some will work in given situations as sermons. Usually the tales challenge the congregation toward service or toward giving. All are educational in some way.

Different groups will use the various offerings in different formats. Some writings will guide us more than once and in a variety of formats. Sometimes using a writing in two or three different formats is helpful. This can be done in a single setting or on separate occasions.

What Do We Get From Stories?

As I prepare this book I have made a difficult assumption. It seems to me most pastors know their own congregations better than I know them. Pastors can probably develop the appropriate format. Every pastor has knowledge of their own congregation and its patterns. Preparing such an event with the aid of several members will best serve most pastors.

I say this is a difficult assumption for good reason. My normal human ego says I know more than does anyone else about everything. Still, this is a tragic error in storytelling. One person can never legitimately say this to another person: "This is what this story means to you!"

In a class at the University of Puget Sound I flunked a basic course. The instructor made a practice of saying, "This is what this story means...."

I responded with, "It may mean that to you. It does not mean that to me. You do not know and cannot know what it means to me." I flunked the course but won the argument, eventually. Each group or individual may or may not take my format suggestions seriously. They are suggestions. Match them against the group as best you see the need. Then take your own responsibilities.

Pastors and other worship leaders have a special challenge as we lay out the words and format for a faith experience. The liturgical crew can only throw the words, actions, and music into the wind. Words and actions cannot be withdrawn once the congregation has witnessed them. Pastor, choir, musicians, ushers, and participants all become prisoners of the service. What we have said and acted upon is complete. No one can change the past.

This captivity can be bitter. We are dealing with the relationships of human beings with each other and with their Creator. These relationships are where people hurt. Worship leaders must understand we can and do shape struggling human lives through our designs. Our words and actions in worship will change our marriages, business relationships, careers, and every other relationship.

I have discovered an interesting corollary to this truism. If one is serious about the Holy Spirit, storytelling works best. No person can, or should, take responsibility for another's thoughts. No pastor should take responsibility for the work of the Spirit. Allow room for the Spirit to do its own work. The only person to take this challenge is the third person of the trinity.

At one point in my pastoral career my district superintendent spied on me. He came to the church after the service had started. The place to watch and listen was from the kitchen, behind folding doors. Eventually, I sensed him back there, but he did not know that I knew.

After the service, he chastised me royally. "That was terrible. How can the people know what to think if the pastor does not tell them? He must be the expert at the pulpit and in the hearts of the congregation."

We did not do very well together after that. I would not push the Lord aside. Staying out of the path of the Spirit in the hearts of the congregation seems best. If God wants to put something in the hearts of the congregation, it will happen. I will do the best I can to support and facilitate. I will study. I will write. I will pray about myself and the people. I will let God use me. I will not make psychological and spiritual demands of the congregation.

At some point, the sermon must become the message of the Lord for the people of the Lord. Then the Bible will make sense. Jesus will make sense. Marriage will make sense. Family and community will make sense. In other words, God will take over. Then Revelation 21 will become a reality: "Then I saw a new heaven and a new earth."

Mistakes will happen. The liturgist or the pastor or the choir will say the wrong word. The organist will play a wrong note sometime. An usher will step on the toe of the church matriarch. After the liturgist or the pastor has committed the deed, nothing can change it. Forgiveness for the past is now up to the Lord. We praise a majestic deity. This God has created the sun and planets and stars and all the rest. God can probably handle "debts" in place of "trespasses."

Perhaps that wrong word or banner is what God had in mind all along for someone in the congregation. It might be God's choice for the pastor or liturgist.

Take these offerings. Use them in ways you think best. Use them for study groups. Tear them apart and reassemble them. Compare them to your own life stories. Make them fit your needs.

Then, when you have mastered something, write your own message and use it. Write your own prayer or psalm or story. Let the Lord use your skill to deliver the divine message.

As you do this, feel the power of the priesthood of all believers. This power comes not from the individual human but from the Spirit of God. All other support is weak.

Lastly, do not shy away from tales of the wampus cat and the sidehill gouger. The wampus cat has a big tail, similar to a telephone pole. Just when we think it is turning to run away it is only turning its tail to us so it can wamp us in the head.

The sidehill gouger has four legs. The two on the left are longer than those on the right. It can only run on slopes, and it can run only sideways. They are very vicious. If one is chasing you, just turn and run up or down the hill or the other way around the hill.

I have known Christians similar to these critters. Enjoy.

The Revised Common Lectionary

The selections posted for each writing are within the Revised Common Lectionary (RCL). Many faith groups within Christianity use the RCL.

The RCL has several values for those who use it. First, it provides a loose bond for Christians of many groups. One may attend a house of worship that is not one's own, and use of the RCL should help eliminate a sense of alienation while visiting.

It provides an assurance that corporate congregational life will address most portions of scripture. The preacher may only read them privately during worship preparation. Even so, they will still leave their mark.

Any lectionary forces the preacher to teach the scriptures in some way. Many pastors ignore this portion of the call. They do so at their own risk.

Almost everyone is free to use any of the various readings suggested in the RCL or any other lectionary. No mandatory lessons attach themselves to any offerings of this book. As a worship leader, you may attach any writing to any portion you choose. If you attach these writings to other portions, please let me know your insight. My mind is always curious about your tools. I am also eager to receive your own sermons and writings used in congregational life. Send them to me at karl4life@aol.com. Thank you, in advance, for helping me.

Personally, I try to work each lectionary reading into the liturgy in some way. An hour of worship provides much room for scripture. The worship may include Old Testament and non-gospel New Testament portions in many ways.

Most of the psalms provide splendid praise and prayer sections. Some psalms make great children's time or lead-ins to prayer. Life guidelines such as the Ten Commandments offer meditation before worship. Many stories and writings offer welcoming words and departing thoughts. The wisdom literature guides us through periods of needed introspection. The possibilities seem to be endless. A free flow of scripture within the service will be a way to cooperate with God. It is God who must finally shape your congregation according to God's own plan. Give God that opportunity.

For Christians, the key portion of scripture for worship is the gospel. I believe we should read the gospel aloud at every worship service. It is the core of every discussion group and any other gathering of Christians. This is the only universally mandated portion of the service. Without a reading of the gospel, I am uncomfortable. I need the reality of the praise, the personal prayer, and the open pronouncements. The lack of these seems to reflect sentiments that are potentially not those of Christ.

Reading the gospel of Jesus, the Christ, is a very special time in Christian worship. As a culture, we have many other similar occasions in our lives. We salute the flag with the pledge of allegiance. If the stars and stripes moves past us in a parade, we stand and place our hand over our heart.

In a court of law, we stand and swear to "tell the truth, the whole truth, and nothing but the truth." Then we sit.

In our homes or in various informal gatherings, when an older person or a more honored person enters, we stand.

Do we dare stand for these, yet fail to stand when to hear the gospel read? Do we not honor the gospel? Do we believe the gospel is less than truth? Is it less important than the flag? Standing for the gospel of Jesus, the Christ, seems appropriate, at the very least.

An Open Book

This book is for everyone. Although I have formatted this book for congregational use, I hope families, individuals, and non-religious groups will use it as well. We encourage pastors to tell your congregations about the book and how it might be helpful to them and their families.

Reading the lectionary material alone or in congregations, faith groups, or families, is critical. I suggest reading each of the lectionary selections before reading the writing itself. This brief period should help move you to enter a zone of peace and readiness for growth in your faith. Following this with a brief prayer for illumination should be productive, as well.

Editor's Note

These stories have been printed as close to the original format as possible to maintain the proper "flavor" and integrity.

Rebecca K. Allen

Response To An Inspirational Story

Personal Or Group Study Guide

Every story experience helps us grow. We change while we listen. The storyteller and listeners will hear these stories together. Posing questions for an individual or for a group is helpful. Give everyone a chance to answer the questions. These queries should promote faith growth.

No right way or wrong way to comprehend these stories exists. No right or wrong answers exist for these questions. Only personal and group statements in response to the writings have any value. Each person's statement is as appropriate as another's.

I should make one concept very plain. None of these stories — nor any story that I write — will ever be written or told just to make a particular point. This would corrupt storytelling as a healing ministry. Every person who hears the story is free to find whatever one needs inside the story. Consider the gospels. Given the same stories, how is it possible that we have so many interpretations of their meaning? If the hearer is open to the action of the Holy Spirit, the teller must necessarily allow the Spirit unlimited room to work. Telling a story to make some specific point is completely wrong, a violation of Christ, and a waste of time.

The story experience should provide growth both individually and in your relationships with others. The personal investment of each participant is critical. This is the driving force toward making lives better.

Spend as much time on these topics as you wish. Do not be afraid of silence in these discussions. Ideas often spring from seeds planted much earlier. A return to these topics later is very proper.

Each person should work through and answer each topic. Writing down all the responses is not important. However, formatting a response in the heart is important for each participant. Listing the study topics below on a poster board for the entire group to see should aid the process.

Encouraging each participant to respond within the time structure of the event is good. The group may require reminding that the structure works only when each person has their own opportunity to respond. Some may wish to "hog" the time. This is most unmannerly in faith study groups.

These topics make good studies for most groups. Discussing the validity, meaning, and value of the questions will help us understand the process of listening to stories, which center around the life and teachings of Christ. As we then experience the tales, we will experience their validity, meaning, and value as we search for new life in Christ.

Study topics:

1. Retell the story in your own words. If in a group, you may wish to share your story.

    Remember: Anyone's version is as right as any other's. In matters of our own heart, we have no elite authorities.

2. Retell the story as if the event occurred today.

    Remember: The story is a slice of a particular time. Try to avoid reading the expectations of one period into a tale of another time.

3. What event in your own life is similar to this narrative? What does that event mean as we look back — or ahead — to it? How is the story a valid representation of the truth of your own event?

    Remember: Each person is unique in their response to past, present, and future history.

4. When we listen to a story, we usually identify with one or more character(s) in the story. Who do you identify with as you listen? Where is your heart? Why and how?

    Remember: Each person is unique and valuable in the whole scope of history. No one can legitimately say to another story witness, "The story must be heard this way."

5. Discuss the other stated characters within the story. Talk about their style, their personality, their hopes, and their dreams.

    Remember: History merges the lives of all the people of the world, yet each is unique and remains that way.

6. Discuss any implied characters in the narrative. Are there unseen and unmentioned individuals or groups of people that have an impact on the events? Who are they and what is their impact on events? Do you identify with any of them?

    Remember: Even the least known persons in history are critically important. Think of the cleaning maid at the inn where Mary went to give birth to Jesus.

7. How should we change the narrative? What changes in personnel could we make to bring this about?

    Remember: Our values shape the way we envision the future.

8. What actions or images or tools in the story hold particular importance for you? What are the signs that something is important to you?

    Remember: Each of us sees historic events from the perspective of different experiences and expectations.

9. What does this narrative mean to you? Are you comfortable with whatever meaning it has for you?

    Remember: This experience is about positive change in our lives and relationships.

10. Does this narrative change anything in your understanding of yourself and your relationship with others? Is it valuable? Is it positive?

Remember: When we look at things that will change our lives, they threaten us. Sometimes they empower our vision of reality in the future.

The life of Jesus of Nazareth touches every life at every moment. Thinking clearly about that impact on our own life and relationships is most important. We can best do that by studying his impact on those around him 2,000 years ago. We can and do search for clues to his own personality, his thinking, his relationships.

In the story experience, we apply our standard questions to stories. Many of the best stories are of Jesus and his close friends. We call these stories "gospel." These seem to provide the best values for our lives.

New Hope
United Methodist Church

Synopsis: The churchyard of a Georgia United Methodist congregation offers hope to a faithful congregation and community.

Liturgical Calendar: Advent 2, Cycle B, any baptism

Scriptures: Isaiah 40:1-11; Psalm 85:1-2, 8-13; 1 Corinthians 1:3-9; Mark 13:24-37

Comment: A true story. The use of seashells in baptism is a good tradition.

Just south of Monticello, Georgia, is a church I dearly love. New Hope Church is a small congregation serving a rolling rural area of southwestern Jasper County.

My family and I served this congregation as one of seven churches on the Shady Dale circuit from 1968-1970. The rolling hills and forested lands were a precious gift from the Creator to me. Each visit to that building and its grounds gave me new reason to love God's genius.

The people of New Hope were intelligent, kind, and generous. Because New Hope was more than twenty miles from our home in Shady Dale, I sometimes came late to the service. Sometimes I led a service in another church several miles away before going to New Hope. If this happened, the congregation would just sing and pray until I reached the church.

The church had another deep blessing. To this day I regret not telling the congregation while I served them just how much I appreciated this special gift they gave me.

Local legend and some history books record that this building served as a field hospital during the Civil War. When General Sherman made his march to the sea, his troops traveled through this area. Before and after the building served his troops, it provided shelter for the Confederate troops and guerilla fighters.

Many of both sides met their death at this site. Others died elsewhere but were brought to New Hope for burial. Some may have been brought in with a vain hope that something could be done to restore their vitality. Most of these fighters were buried in the churchyard at New Hope. Many, though not all, of the Confederate fighters were later given tombstones in the cemetery.

The local people buried the federal soldiers without stones. Most of these graves were not marked. The only notation of these grave sites was a group of shallow pits in the lawn where loose grave soil packed and then settled.

This was only the beginning of my interest in the New Hope churchyard cemetery. For around 200 years, the dead of the European community near the church had been buried there. Prior to these settlers, native peoples for thousands of years buried their dead in the area: farmers and their families, shopkeepers, bootleggers, everyone.

Donella and I visited the grounds just a few days after moving to the area. When we walked around the grounds, our first image was of many special grave sites.

These special sites were the burial places of children under the age of six. The concrete slab laid over the grave to keep out wild animals was about six inches thick. Most of the slabs were rounded over. The concrete was then covered with perfect clam or oyster shells turned over and pressed into the wet concrete.

We eventually had to ask some local folks about the shells. There was a very simple explanation. The shell is an ancient sign of Christian baptism. Traditionally, holy water was dipped from a bowl by the pastor using a perfect clam or other seashell. All these children had apparently been baptized. One or two local people suggested that the children might not have been baptized. Most local folks thought it had been done.

If the end of the world comes, the saints who come to get all the baptized people will know the sense of the child. At least the family wanted the child baptized, whether that happened or not.

Many of these burials occurred during the flu epidemics of 1915-1920.

This set of graves in the New Hope churchyard gives me renewed hope for the world. In this one small field lay fathers and mothers, children and teens. There are soldiers for both sides of a terrible war. These were treated for their wounds in the church. Food and bandages were brought by local people if any supplies were available. Both before and after, the church filled its role as an icon of the cycle of life.

A few years ago, the building burned to the ground from a lightning hit. The congregation rebuilt the church for the community. The church serves on, serving as it has for many generations. There will be more graves, more baptisms, more marriages, more birthday parties.

I hope some other pastor will have the great privilege I have had with this congregation. I held my own daughter in one arm and a cute little red-headed toddler in the other while bringing a message of God's peace and new life to this congregation. Let us also pray for no more need to bury soldiers killed in combat.

Angie

Synopsis: A young mother struggles to support her disabled husband and children. Suicide beckons.

Liturgical Calendar: Christmas Sunday, New Year, Cycles A, B, C

Scriptures: Ecclesiastes 3:1-13; Psalm 8; Revelation 21:1-6a; Matthew 25:31-46

Comment: A true story. Once delivered as an ordination sermon.

US Highway 101 in the night rain is very dark and dangerous. From the Olympic Peninsula to Tijuana, it can be a wild ride. US 101 can trap the driver with slick roads and dangerous curves. The road winds around rock cliffs and sand dunes thrown up by the Pacific. It is not a good road for someone in a hurry. It is especially not a good road for any driver whose mind is somewhere else.

Late one night, I drove north along the Oregon Coast from Florence toward Yachats. The truck sheltered me well from the rain and the wind. My little pickup was almost a castle in the storm. I was glad I didn't make my living on the small crabbing boats. Mucking up crustaceans from the ocean floor might be more suicidal than productive.

The wind was blowing spray up onto the highway from the waves crashing below. Visibility was so bad most cars were crawling along the cliff highway. Twenty or thirty miles per hour was standard. Sometimes I would see a driver hunched over a steering wheel. We all struggled to see through the rain pounding on our windshield. The wipers were almost irrelevant at any speed. These curves and cliffs were dangerous. Even those of us who drove this route often knew our peril.

The old Chevy pickup parked near the rail on the ocean side almost looked "at home" in the weather. The wind and rain from the storm seemed to beat on the doors and windows without success. It should have been a safe haven for anyone. The wispy figure of a young woman was leaning on the guardrail taking the full blast of the storm. She needed the safety and shelter of a truck.

She made no motion of any kind as I stopped and backed toward her pickup. Nosed into the wind, my truck seemed secure. It escaped having the door pulled off by an eighty miles per hour wind from behind.

I pulled on my slicker and pushed back against the storm to get to her. No one sat in her pickup.

She wore jeans and tenny-runners and a windbreaker, all of which were soaked through with salty rain. Her long golden-blonde hair was matted around her head from wind and rain. Her eyes were fixed on the waves below slamming themselves and the logs and boards they carried against the rocks.

"Are you all right?" No answer.

"Can I help? Is your pickup broke down?" Still no answer. I wrapped my plastic slicker around both of us. She did not attempt to object or to fit herself into the slicker.

"Maybe we need to talk. Let's go sit in my pickup so we don't both freeze out here." Stumbling over the rail to a violent end was likely in this wind.

I half carried her along. She allowed me to steer her to my pickup. She did not protest as I pushed her inside. I chose to fasten her seatbelt. Perhaps I was afraid she would try to jump out and climb over the guardrail.

In the pickup I turned the heater on high. I pulled an old shirt from behind the seat and used it to try to dry her face and hair. While I wiped the storm from her face I told her about myself. She should not be afraid of me, I thought. She probably did not hear a word of it. I told her who I was and what I was doing in the area. It was several minutes before she spoke.

"I'm cold."

"You'll be all right now. We'll have you warm in no time. Live over in the valley?"

With some encouragement, for the next half hour she told me about herself. Sometimes her words rambled. Sometimes she

29

startled me with her clarity and force. Sometimes spaces of a minute or two came between words. Always in my mind was the big question. Why?

Angie had married young. It was a good marriage. Bert was her childhood sweetheart. He loved her deeply and worked hard to provide her and their two little girls with a good home. Bert drove a company log truck out of Prineville. He worked the massive pine and fir forests within a couple hundred miles. It was a good life. Bert was proud of his work and his family. Angie was proud of Bert. She supported him in every way she could. Angie was also happy with her own ability to raise two beautiful children in a good home.

Bert and Angie even dreamed of the day they could have a log truck of their own, contracting the work. They spent many hours figuring out just what truck they wanted. They even planned the date of purchase. It seemed the ideal life might one day be theirs.

Almost.

One Saturday, Bert had an accident at home. He fell while lifting something. He pulled muscles and damaged his vertebrae. It was not terribly serious, except that he could no longer drive a truck. Something about the way he had to twist his muscular body caused problems. Driving required him to step on the clutch and slam the gear levers simultaneously.

Bert finally recovered enough that he could stay home and care for the girls. The company wanted to help them in every way it could. When Angie applied for Bert's old job driving a log truck, they gave it to her. The community was a tight family. Bert and Angie were important to them. Now she had the chance to make the good money Bert had always made before.

Angie had often ridden with Bert. He liked her company, and she could help with the work. She could keep up the paper work and help him with chains. When Bert drove, she made it part of her own work to keep the windshield and inside the cab clean.

Now she had all the responsibility. Angie fought with chains, come-alongs, snow, diesel fuel, and bad roads. It was good money, though definitely not the kind of job she would have preferred.

Truck driving was hard on her small body. The equipment wasn't the best, and the bad roads and long hours beat mercilessly on her small body. She knew she eventually would be forced to find some other work. A truck with better power steering would have helped. She also needed a smoother transmission and better shocks. She couldn't take much more of this.

Then the recession came. Angie was about ready to quit, but the company laid her off instead. The layoff helped because she could draw unemployment for half a year. She would be out of luck when that ran out.

After several months of searching for work, Angie took a job with a state office in Prineville. The state had one condition. She had to learn again to type. She had worked a short time in an office when she and Bert first married. This new job might be a godsend.

When Angie brought out the old family typewriter to practice, she knew she could not use it. She found that her brief struggle with steel and rubber had jammed her fingers and wrists. The months in the truck severely damaged her hands. She could not flex them enough for typing. On top of that, Angie's back was now beat up from the old truck seat. The seat was too large to fit her. Now she could not sit in an office chair for more than a half hour without excruciating pain. No way could she qualify for the office job that awaited her.

The unemployment checks were ending. Bert was still getting his disability, but Social Security cutbacks were threatening those benefits.

Finally, the word came that the Social Security Disability was finished entirely. That same day Angie drew her last unemployment check.

Angie and Bert sat at the table that evening writing checks. They paid those bills they could pay. Finally they had only $40 left in the world. Their life together, which once seemed so complete, looked completely empty ahead.

The following morning, Bert was still asleep from the medication he took for his pain. Angie had not closed her eyes all night. When she rose, Angie checked the day's clothing for the girls. Angie kissed them quietly in the dark. She climbed slowly into the old faithful pickup. At the station she bought $20 worth of gas. In the early light, she headed west across Santiam Pass and the Coast Range.

Angie stopped a few times to catch a quick nap and to think a little. She took twelve hours to make a five-hour trip. Angie's destination was not clear in her mind. She only knew she needed to drive. As she drove, her desperation grew more violent with each mile and each minute.

Blinded by fear and rage, she stopped. She sat there for a moment, nearly sick with rage. She raged at the system, at herself, and at God. She parked on a wide spot on the road near a guardrail. She left the keys in the pickup and walked to the rail. Standing at the edge, Angie slowly allowed herself to become caught up in the roar of the surf. She watched the logs being smashed to bits on the rocks below. Eventually, she began to feel she was already down there among them.

She deserved the pain. She could already feel herself pounding against the rocks by the surf. The beating would pay her back for leaving her family. It would be just desserts for spending half of their last dollars for her own end.

Angie was loosening her grip on the rail. She was ready to make herself one with the waves and the rocks below her. Then she found herself guided by something new, a different sound.

"Are you all right? Can I help you?"

When Angie reached this point in her story she became irate. She jumped from the pickup and slammed the door. I got out and ran around to her side, grabbing her around the waist. I held tight to avoid what I thought might happen next.

"You stopped me. I could have done it. It would be over by now. You should mind your own business!"

She slapped me hard across the face. She beat on my chest with her fists and kicked my shins hard enough to draw blood.

Then she cried. Big sobs and huge tears added to the rain and seawater already cascading down her face. We stood there in the roar of the storm and the surf for about twenty minutes. Angie slowly relaxed a little. Perhaps it was a bit of resignation. Then she simply pulled open the door of my pickup. I let her get inside.

We drove back into Yachats, a few miles up the road. The little bar there was still open. We spent a couple hours drinking coffee. The barkeeper that night was still struggling with her own husband's layoff some time earlier. She was probably more understanding than I. She took Angie in the back and put a dry shirt on her and helped her get warm.

Angie told us most of the story again. She began to talk more about the girls, about Bert, and about their friends in Prineville.

When the time came for the bar to close, I suggested calling some of my friends in Yachats. I knew they would put her up for the night. Or, if she liked, I could put her up in a motel for the night.

Angie said that she thought she wanted to go home. This bothered me a lot. She might be a real danger to herself. I knew whatever she did must be her choice. Perhaps she had worked some things out in her system and could make it now. I just did not know.

I took her back to her old Chevy pickup and followed her on to Florence. At an all-night station, we bought her some gas. I made a quick check of her tires and oil.

Just before Angie drove away, she stepped out of the pickup to readjust the seat and the mirrors. I put an arm around her to give her a hug.

Angie turned her shoulder to me, wouldn't let me get close. I asked her to call me or write me to let her know how she was doing. She turned toward the Chevy, then back toward me. She buried her face in my shoulder, and again she cried.

After two or three minutes she finally quieted down. She looked at me for an instant. Then Angie did a very strange thing. She turned completely around in my arms. She smiled a quick little happy smile and turned around again, even doing a little dance about it. Maybe it was a little dance of freedom.

Then she looked at me with those once-again shining eyes. "I've never known what it would be to stand in the arms of a loving God."

33

Then she was gone, driving the old pickup off into the sunrise. I prayed she would make it back to Prineville, back to Bert and to Tina and Lisa. I wanted her to go back to her life. As the pickup chugged out of town through the wind and the rain, I said a little prayer for all the Angies of the world.

Serving From The Bell Tower
Is Not Easy

Synopsis: Is a country church bell tower the best place to carry out one's ministry? Perhaps not.

Liturgical Calendar: July 17-23, Proper 11, Ordinary Time 16, Cycle C

Scriptures: Amos 8:1-12; Psalm 52 or 82; Colossians 1:15-28; Luke 10:38-42

Comment: A true story.

The ladder leading to the bell tower looked risky, at best. The boards climbed the wall of the Shedd Church entry. It posed a challenge for any who would climb to the bell landing.

That bell tower satisfied a need inside my soul. Sometimes in the summer I could bring a book along to help me revive my weary soul. With my back against a corner post I read or slept or consciously meditated for many hours. This pattern ended abruptly after only a few days.

The bishop had sent us to Shedd, a small farming community. The congregation was stable but growing slightly. This church had no significant money problems. The members had a strong sense of national and international missions.

This summer, the largest problem they had was their source of income. Most grew grass seed on their Willamette Valley farms. After harvest, they burned the field to prevent bacterial growth in the straw.

Burning was expensive and dangerous. The farmers and the universities looked for other ways to rid themselves of the straw and the bacteria. No one could find a better solution. Some people who settled in the valley after the grass seed industry rose were adamant. The industry must stop its pollution. The smoke caused asthma, auto accidents, and dirty windows. It was not as bad as cigarette smoke, but many considered cigarette smoking a public right.

Someone began to burn the unharvested fields and the large seed cleaner buildings. Before the seed is combined or harvested, it must lay in the field for several days to dry. After a few days, it is particularly vulnerable to fire. The arsonist simply torched fields after they were cut and before they were harvested.

The arsonist also began to set fire bombs in the large seed cleaner warehouses of the community. Eight or ten bombs were set in the warehouses. Two actually destroyed buildings and equipment. The owners discovered the others before they could do their full damage. Most of the damage came at night.

I wanted desperately to help the community stop this evil. Very quickly, I saw that I might climb that ladder into the bell tower to use as a watching post. From it I could see almost every road within two or three miles of Shedd. I could also see any flames that came from burning fields or buildings in the area. Aha!

One evening I climbed to my post. With small binoculars, I watched carefully for vehicles moving about. Only a few came and went along those country roads. Getting a license plate number seemed an easy task, but I still had a problem.

If I saw a car moving past the church, or saw flames spreading, I had to climb down the ladder. My eyes and binoculars were not powerful enough to see license plates from the tower. This made it necessary to climb down the ladder and hustle out the door of the church to the street, and this must be done before the vehicle was gone from the area.

After several wasted attempts to get license numbers, I realized this was not going to work. From the tower I could see the flames and the vehicles as I expected. To really do anything important, though, being at ground level was critical. Finally, that night, I gave up trying to accomplish anything from the tower. I simply sat on the steps of the church. With a pencil and notebook I recorded any license numbers and vehicle descriptions for several hours. Nothing much really came of these efforts. No fires started in the area while I sat out on the church steps.

However, his changed my preaching pattern. Christian ministry cannot be practiced from a tower position. Occasionally I found time to go into the tower for renewal and study. For direct contact with the congregation or community, ground level was necessary. Even Jesus made his work among the lowest of the low in his society. If we are to serve as he did, it must be done at ground level.

The Gentle Circle Of Aidan

Synopsis: Suggesting a gentle Christianity. Aidan became the chief missionary to Northumberland, formerly known as Northumbria, the area between England and Scotland.

Liturgical Calendar: Epiphany 4, Cycle A

Scriptures: Micah 6:1-8; Psalm 15; 1 Corinthians 1:18-31; Matthew 5:1-12

Comment: A true story. Aidan's life laid the groundwork for later development of Presbyterianism in the northern isles.

Missionary, Abbot, Bishop of Lindisfarne
(Born Ireland: 605; died: 31 August 651)

AD 635 was a tough time to be alive in Europe. The continent was crashing into the darkest of the Dark Ages. It was the beginning of some evil and cruel times. People of all groups existed only at the will of the latest conqueror.

This hard life in Europe helped our world in some ways. It opened the door to faith over the ashes of worldly authority. The changing tides of European history soon trashed many rulers.

World travel became a reality. African, Scandinavian, and Asian cultures traveled to the Americas. Writing down and preserving the thoughts of ordinary people became important. Folks began to see the worth of other people and the dreams of other nations.

Meanwhile, many ideas of those years hurt the world. The groundwork for the crusades began to take shape as Islam spread over the Mediterranean. The clashes of Islam, Judaism, and Christianity even today have their roots in the turmoil of European and African history. Even the history of American slavery traces this disaster through the disrespect for peoples of the Dark Ages.

Some dark ages live on today. The notion arose that only a specially trained and ordained person could properly open the Bible to others. This dark spot on the spirit of the reformation has hurt all of Christ's churches.

The intent of this practice is to control the lives of those who would be faithful to Jesus. The Roman Catholic church of the 1400s, 1500s, and 1600s openly struggled to protect this authority. The church hit hard at those who tried to bypass this code. Popes demanded death for Luther, Calvin, and many others in this quarrel. These fathers tried to think outside the box of institutional control.

Today, the ego of professional religious elitism lives on. That notion exists as much in Protestantism as in Catholicism. The chief proponents are a few sectarian groups. Most of these groups go one of two paths. They either reject trained clergy altogether, or they set up their own schools to teach their own clergy. Many have tried to move past these bounds.

Aidan of Lindisfarne was one whose life moved past the chains of his day. His words and actions paved the way for the practice of mutual support and guidance. The Presbyterian movement eventually adopted his guidelines within the faith.

Presbyterian tradition in the isles is a product of more than a thousand years of faithful labor. The tradition of faithful search and service was honored and continued by the clergy and laity of the northern isles. The churches of Scotland and Northumbria worked their way through many struggles.

One peasant leader of this search was a young Irish monk, Aidan. His spirit lives on in the dreams of the group, if not in all its practices. Aidan was one of those of human society who seem destined to move the world. When the young monk came to the foreground, Christianity was a hit-or-miss scattering around Scotland. When he died, the faith was well on the way to acceptance within the religious structure of the area.

The gospel first became the general faith of the northern areas around 627. In that year, King Edwin of Northumbria converted from a local religion to Christianity. He heard a presentation led by Bishop Paulinus of Canterbury. After Edwin came to follow Jesus, Paulinus made his home at York. A severe pagan revolt followed Edwin's death in battle in 632. This wiped out much of the work of Edwin and Paulinus.

A year later, Edwin's exiled nephew, Oswald, returned to the land ready for battle. He won back the kingdom in war. As king, he restored the Christian mission. This eventually became the core sense of the Presbyterian movement. Under his leadership, community discussion and mutual support became core portions of Christian processes in the northern isles.

During his exile, Oswald had lived at Columba's monastery of Iona — a stronghold of mission work. There he converted and offered himself for baptism. After becoming king, he sent to Iona for missionaries rather than to Canterbury.

The first monk to respond was Corman. Poor Corman had no success and no clue. He returned to Iona discouraged. The custom for travelers at Iona was a public debriefing immediately upon returning. It was, and is, the same at most churches and mission groups. This brings news from far lands. The bishop invited Corman to speak to the others gathered in the longhouse.

He began by remembering his own call to discipleship. He spoke of his own eager passion to spread the knowledge of Christ to people everywhere. When the bishop asked Corman to go to Northumbria it was as if he were headed to the moon. He assumed this hundred miles or so would place him in a world vastly different from anything he had known.

It was that and more. Corman assumed the common position of royal conversion advocates. That is, when a king converted to a faith, the entire nation converted. The requirement for a missionary was to only air out the notions of the new faith. Then, supposedly, the people would gladly buy into the new theology. The missionary was the welcome hero to the nation because the king wanted it so.

This idea, however, just did not work in Northumbria. The people did not follow the king. Thankfully, King Oswald saw things apparently far advanced for his time. He understood that the really important portion of faith is what happens between the heart of the individual and Christ. The second portion is the relationship between individuals in the shadow of Christ. Oswald allowed people to come to Christ in their own ways.

Corman could not swallow this. He seemed to have assumed Oswald would evangelize by force. Corman thought Oswald would force the nation to accept Corman's teaching. Oswald did not force the issue. The strong king honored personal commitment and sensitivities.

The people rejected Corman's heavy-handed approach. Corman loudly complained that the Northumbrians were a savage and unteachable people. To Corman, they were that, and much worse.

Aidan, a young Irish monk, listened carefully to the raging of Corman. The abuse saddened Aidan deeply. When Corman finished, Aidan thought carefully for a time.

Aidan had gained a reputation as a thinker, a wise man. As he sat in the circle of the elders of the faith, he knew others were waiting for his convictions. Finally, Aidan was ready to speak to the scenario laid out by Corman.

Aidan suggested that Corman might have been too harsh with his listeners. He knew how the people struggled with the cruelty of royalty. As he sat with his faithful community, Aidan heard their desperation. Their scars were not just from battles with invading Europeans and Scandinavians. The people also bore the marks of royal whips and lances.

Aidan asked Corman, "Did you perhaps not first give them the sweet milk of the simple truth of Jesus?" He added, "Perhaps you were too harsh with them. They might have responded better to a gentler approach."

At this, the bishop appointed Aidan to lead a second mission to Northumbria as bishop in 635. The bishop appointed Aidan, at his own request, to Lindisfarne. Lindisfarne is a part-time island off the northeast coast of Northumbria. Twice each day, at high tides, the waters cut the island off from the mainland.

The locals have often called this the Holy Isle. Aidan built a small monastery and chapel on the island.

At Lindisfarne he set up the rule of Saint Columban. Bede says, "It was a beautiful sight. The bishop (who was only learning English) preached. Then the king and his officers translated for the people. The royal party learned English during their long exile in Scotland."

King Oswald was also wise enough to know that the words of the bishop were good. However, the people would give them more acceptance if they came from the mouth of the king. So the words of Aidan became the words of Oswald.

Oswald was a gentle man himself. The people and his peers highly respected him. The respect for Oswald only added to the good natured support for the notions of Aidan. The people responded with admiration and support for both men.

King Oswald often served as Aidan's interpreter. Aidan gathered his fellow monks and the English youths whom he trained. Together they returned Christianity to Northumbria. They took the mission through the land as far south as London.

Bede says that "Nothing of Aidan was more hopeful to the people than that Aidan lived as he taught. He looked to nothing for himself which belonged to this world. The king often gave him food and clothing, even lands. He quickly gave these to the poor."

"Aidan always traveled on foot when he could. Wherever he saw any person, either rich or poor, he invited them in some way. If they were pagans, he encouraged them to embrace the mystery of the faith." (Christ has died. Christ has risen. Christ will come again.)

"If those he met were believers, he worked to strengthen them in their faith. He tried to stir them up by his own words and actions. In their lives, Aidan gave us many lives of good works."

Aidan died August 31, 651, at Bamborough, the royal town. He was apparently brokenhearted at the death of his king, Oswald.

King Oswald, the gentle patron of Christianity in Northumbria, died twelve days earlier in a minor revolution. This act was part of the deep turmoil that was the Dark Ages.

The Roman church martyrology lists Aidan's name on August 31.

Bishop Andrew —
The Bishop's Sacrifice

Synopsis: Bishop Andrew struggles between satisfying the requirements of the denomination and the wishes of two slave children.

Liturgical Calendar: Epiphany 8, Cycle C

Scriptures: Isaiah 55:10-13; Psalm 92:1-4, 12-15; 1 Corinthians 15:51-58; Luke 6:39-49

Comment: A true story. This event has been a source of controversy for a century-and-a-half. Understanding it is very important to the whole church.

James Andrew did not sleep much these days.

Whatever he did seemed wrong. James Andrew was in a position of hurt. He was frustrated at finding himself the central personality in a developing split in the church. His frustration was all the worse for living with realities he could not control.

James was a bishop in the Methodist church, and it was General Conference time. Once in each four years the church met to work out its life. Typically, it chose its goals and organization for the future. This year the problems at hand overwhelmed the conference.

Never had the church struggled harder with itself than it did right now. In these few days of the 1844 General Conference, debate was bitter. The conference met at the Green Street Church in New York City. This was not a likely spot for an earthshaking event.

James really did not feel internally as he thought a bishop of the church ought to feel. He was not a man to use powerful oratory. He did not often condemn the sins of the world with threats of fire and eternal damnation. This man of God even had difficulty telling preachers where to go to preach. The powerful bishop was always self-conscious concerning his own failings.

This quiet man was really a pastor first, last, and always. Bishop Andrew felt most comfortable in quiet conversations, one-on-one. If someone needed a friend, the bishop was available. He knew he was in the right place when someone came to ask about Jesus. Talking about the impact of his Lord on his and others' lives was a great release for a troubled life.

He was comfortable visiting in the homes of the people of his parish. Sometimes he began his visits in the early morning and continued until late in the evening. Through the day, he talked with his pastors. Lay folks in his parish and many strangers found him on the streets. Sometimes he sat in a small café drinking tea or coffee, hoping someone would sit with him for conversation.

It was this thought about visiting with the people of his parish that troubled him. It was this thought that brought him back to the source of his worry. The people of his parish well knew his love. The people whom Andrew knew, and loved, and longed to be with, were both black and white.

More than that, two of them he legally owned and could not set free. They were literally his slaves. The bishop had papers that said he owned them. For this he wept. He cried for them and for himself.

Mony, the pretty young girl, was a daughter to him. In her teens, she had been a gift to the bishop from an elderly lady from Augusta. Mony came with a specific condition. When she reached sixteen, she would be freed. Passage to Liberia, the nation set aside in Africa for freed slaves, would be set aside for her.

Mony refused to go. When she reached sixteen, she chose to remain in America as the slave of a kind and loving man. Her potential freedom in Africa held little hope for her.

Mony knew if she accepted freedom in America she would be in a worse position. If she were freed, she risked falling into the hands of kidnappers and possibly made a slave again. This time, her position would probably be much worse. She could easily become a sex slave to an abusive man or woman.

Mony chose to stay with the bishop at least until she found a husband. That, in itself, was all right with the bishop, although he wished she could, and would, accept freedom.

Bishop Andrew was perhaps too kind. He could not bring himself to force her out of his house. He occasionally talked with her about her reasons for being unwilling to leave. He even offered to give her the papers of freedom and let her stay on in his home.

Mony wanted to avoid that. She also had the correct fear that some violent slave merchant might be her new master. The attractive young woman would go to another part of the South and be reduced to slavery again. Someone could rape her and force her into pregnancy. Many slave-producing plantations eagerly searched for women such as her. She could be kept in pregnancy until she could no longer produce. Then she would be no more than a field hand.

Perhaps she would be forced to work in the fields while pregnant. This was the usual case. Anyway, she was better off with Bishop Andrew.

Jon, the boy, was now twelve years old. Bishop Andrew's first wife, now dead, had owned the boy from birth. The bishop loved Jon in the same way that he would have loved his own son. They spent time together walking and talking and considering.

The bishop wanted Jon to be free. The law of the state of Georgia said a male slave could not be set free. No waivers were allowed. Georgia law required that even the few black professional athletes be slaves. If the bishop wanted to rid himself of the slave, Jon, he had to sell the boy.

However, the bishop was convinced he could not sell someone he loved. Even if the bishop did sell Jon, it would end badly. Jon would probably gain a worse life than what he had with the bishop. Field-hand slavery is a violent existence. Jon's life with the Andrews was very comfortable. Bishop Andrew and the bishop's second wife were his family.

So the Andrews chose to educate Jon and Mony in the best ways they could. They taught them to read and write and to do math. Jon and Mony learned history and politics and logic. It was a total violation of the laws of Georgia.

Bishop Andrew believed this to be the best gift they could give the children. It was the best way to prepare them for the freedom that surely would be theirs one day.

45

Bishop Andrew knew a person who could read and write and think must, to some measure, be free. The slave would be free to think. The slave would be free to dream. The slave would be free to see a future as more than the law allowed. The literate slave would know he or she was more than an animal. Whether slave or free, a person has the right to see one's self as more than a beast of burden. No one is just another person's property.

Even with his efforts, he was failing the children. Although he dreamed of setting them free, he could not, at least not yet. The law still recognized them as his property. If he gave them up, they would become the property of the government. Then someone else could buy them.

Although he did not want them as slaves, the law said they were his to buy and sell. These were the only choices available to him now. In earlier years, he could have freed them. Now the state laws had changed. If he freed them, slave agents would likely recapture and charge them with being runaways. The state would whip, brand, and place them in slavery again.

Jon and Mony were his to build up or to destroy. Jon and Mony were his to breed to other slaves if he chose. As slaves, they were not unlike cattle, horses, or pigs. He could build up a stronger herd of slaves if he chose.

His problem was simple. He owned slaves. He was the icon of the bitter struggle within the church. Although he owned them against his will, he owned them.

At that 1844 General Conference, the Committee on Episcopacy held great power over the church. It did not look so much at the needs of individuals. It looked at ways to continue the divisiveness building in the denomination. Building the struggle became a tool in the drive for power and position in the church. The committee for the bishops demanded that Bishop Andrew be relieved of his office and a replacement named. The problem was that he owned slaves.

The Methodist church, through which James Andrew had given his life, was laying its whip on the back of a faithful man. It was living out the truism that much religious activity is done to control the lives of others. Worse, men and women were strengthening their own positions by destroying a bishop of the church.

James Andrew had learned as a boy that God loves everyone, black or white, slave or free, male or female. Now the church refused to find a way to love a man caught by his own love for two black children.

In the Methodist church, James Andrew had come to the conclusion that slavery was wrong and must one day disappear. Now his beloved church was on the brink of humiliating him as a bishop. It limited its own debate to the issue that he was the owner of slaves. It did not matter that he tried to love them and support them as he would have his own children. The conference ignored his protests that he had tried to convince them to leave. He was vulnerable and available. He was the unwilling, though legal, owner of slaves that he treated as his own family.

In the dark of that night, in 1844, Bishop Andrew cried. It was not a cry of bitterness. He was too confused to be bitter. It was the cry of aloneness. Who could he turn to? He had the sense that he had wasted his life. His slaves were crushing all he had tried to do for the kingdom of God. Even his attempts to free his own slaves were failing. The toadies in the denomination were washing away his service and his faith. They only wanted to make a statement that was politically correct.

No one at this General Conference cared about Jon or Mony or about James Andrew. They only cared whether they could destroy Bishop Andrew as a symbol of the South.

James struggled with the eternal questions of the heart. Has it not always been this way — that history knows men and women mostly for their jobs? Has it not always been that the press of daily business and international affairs causes the loss of deep-in-the-heart lives of faithful people? Yes, even the church has not always cared. The church has often put more emphasis on public confessions of faith than on strength of character. Even the church has put more importance on numbers of people rather than on dreams of people.

As Bishop Andrew thought along those lines that spring night, his mind wandered to his second wife. He thought about what this uproar would do to her. He thought about Jon and Mony, his children and his slaves.

Somehow they were now together in the hearts of the family. The bishop, the woman he loved dearly, and the two children were a loving family together. The children felt themselves sacred in the hearts of Christ, as well as the bishop and his wife. Now they were together in pain. James Andrew knew their presence, and they knew his.

James Andrew was at peace with himself. He was comfortable with God, with his wife, and with Jon and Mony.

Somehow another person shared the space. Somehow another was in the room, and the spirit of that presence made the night peaceful.

The next afternoon, the struggle to remain a bishop began in earnest. The Committee on the Episcopacy made its bitter report. It demanded that the conference dismiss Bishop Andrew. The conference could easily appoint another to replace him.

Then, someone made another suggestion. After a lengthy debate, the conference approved this second notion. The conference approved it only because it allowed everyone to claim victory. Sadly, though, it destroyed many years of labor. The leadership saw it as the only possible way to avoid a split in the church. That would have come with the first proposal, and it did come later.

This second concept sent James Andrew back to Georgia as a bishop, but with no post. No episcopal area of the church existed for the bishop to oversee. He was a bishop in name and heart only.

So Bishop Andrew went home to Georgia. He was not a completely defeated man, but close. The bishop lost part of his life in the struggle over slavery. This was a struggle in which no winners could be named for many years yet to come. Yet, Bishop Andrew was not totally defeated.

He returned home to his wife, and to Jon and Mony. He returned to Georgia to live out his years in early retirement. He could continue serving Christ and the church in other ways.

Throughout his life, James Andrew would remember that moment in the upstairs room in the New York hotel. He clearly felt the presence and the touch of the woman he loved. He sensed the presence of Jon and Mony. James knew another presence came into the room with him and brought him new life.

Several years later, the bishop spoke to a small group of friends and recalled the words of Jesus. "If two or three of you struggle with a thing in this life, that will be my struggle as well. Where two or three of you gather together I am with you. When several of you become a community of the faithful, a part of the church, I am there as well" (Matthew 18:8).

Too Much Air

Synopsis: A Georgia bridge is too low. Recovery from disaster requires letting out some excess air.

Liturgical Calendar: Epiphany 4, Cycle C

Scriptures: Micah 6:1-8; Psalm 15; 1 Corinthians 1:18-31; Matthew 5:1-12

Comment: A true story.

The only tow truck in Shady Dale was not large. Junior Champion used it to move cars and small trucks. Large trucks or vehicles that presented heavier pulling problems were a different matter. His little truck just could not do it.

On the south edge of town a railroad crossed the highway on a trestle. The trestle had a clearance of about eleven feet. Local truckers were well aware that this bridge was too low to allow trucks of any size to pass underneath. The locals with high loads simply left the highway and drove along Railroad Street to avoid the matter. Others found different ways to address the matter.

Livestock trucks were the most significant continuing problem for Shady Dale. These beasts were often thirteen feet high. Their drivers were normally young, in a hurry, and operating at night. Several times, some driver obviously made an unfortunate error.

Cruunnnch! Hitting the trestle with a thirteen-foot livestock truck at sixty miles per hour usually had a unique effect. It peeled the top of that trailer back like the lid on a can of sardines from Norway. Then the truck and trailer were stuck under the railroad.

Even if the trailer were loaded with cattle or sheep or pigs the driver had no need to worry about them. The trailer was pinned against the bridge so nothing could climb out or over the top. The truck just could not leave.

When a truck and trailer jammed itself in, someone always contacted Junior. Junior brought his little tow truck to the scene. That was mostly for effect, I suppose. It also enabled him to charge for his time. His truck could not move that tractor and trailer out from under that bridge. He knew it. The entire community knew it.

Junior hemmed and hawed and looked around at the predicament for a time. He waited for the truck driver to become really excited and desperate. By that time, many of us in the community would show up to stand around to watch the outcome and take pictures. This may not have helped the driver, but it was fun. I believe it did help Junior.

Just when the driver was ready to hitchhike back to Monticello to find the sheriff and a larger tow truck, Junior would offer to get the truck unstuck. Then the driver would try anything. Junior and his son, Larry, would go around to each tire and let some air out of each one to lower the trailer three or four inches.

Junior would then suggest that the driver get in the truck and back it out, *after* making the appropriate tow truck service payment, of course. Most drivers were happy to do this. Occasionally, the dolly wheels of the trailer were dropped first. Then some air was let out from the tires of the tractor, and the tractor was driven out. Then the trailer could be lowered and pulled back away from the trestle.

Letting out someone's excess air works wonders, at times.

After all this was over, someone in the crowd spoke loudly the words we all knew to be true. "Someone should have let the air out of that driver before he hit the bridge."

The same is true of many others.

Bullpen Mud

Synopsis: A teenager rescues a tiny puppy from the stumbling hoofs of a large bull. In the process, the teen matures dramatically.

Liturgical Calendar: Epiphany 3, Cycle C

Scriptures: Nehemiah 8:1-10; Psalm 19; 1 Corinthians 12:12-31a; Luke 4:14-21

Comment: A true story — enjoy it.

Growing up on a family dairy farm was wild. It gave me some experiences that I wouldn't trade for anything. Well, almost anything. I would gladly forget some things that happened.

The first act of morning chores was one of the proudest for me. When I was old and sturdy enough to carry it out, I knew I had arrived. Only a man could do this!

We kept the herd bull in a stout log pen close to the barn. He was my special task. I really liked Elmer, and I knew he liked me. Of course, I was very likable. So was he.

Morning and evening, after milking the cows, we fed all the livestock. Usually, it was just me. I had six sisters and a baby brother. In those days, general knowledge found it improper for girls to work hard. Usually the girls divided up the work in the house. I milked the cows, fed all the animals, did much of the irrigating, and harvested most of the crops. Sometimes my sisters helped. Recently one of my sisters said this was not really the case. Now they tell me, fifty years later.

Morning and evening there were chores to do. First, I fed the herd bull, then the cows and steers, then the young animals. Feeding the calves was mostly a nuisance, but it had to be done.

Usually, the herd bull was a fine, well-built ton of purebred Holstein beef. We took special care selecting which calf would be the herd bull. We carefully bought or traded for a young calf with this special duty in mind. He must have large bones and be healthy and be active, but not cranky. He needed to be frisky.

Then we gave the baby herd bull some special attention. We groomed him often. He eventually rewarded us with his own good work. Elmer seemed particularly proud of his efforts. He fathered some very good calves.

Holstein bulls can grow to be quite large. Elmer weighed around a ton and a quarter or so. Huge muscles and bones were the marks of these behemoths. We were very careful to groom them and work closely with them. We wanted them to be comfortable around us. It was important they not become unmanageable. Occasionally, we chose to show the young ones at the county fair. We wanted them to be very tame.

We kept the herd bull in a log pen by himself. This, also, was supposed to be so he would not become wild. However, I knew the truth. We knew what would make him wild. We joked a lot about it. After all, the bulls were not much more than teenagers themselves, and we knew ... we knew.

Sometimes I rode the bull around the pen when my parents weren't watching. Especially, I rode Elmer. The muscles in his back and hips, even as a calf, were almost unbelievable. His legs were sturdy as tree trunks. I had to be careful.

Everyone in the family knew that bulls will be bulls. Simple violence is not out of mind for any of them. No one intends them to be family pets. They are so big! Any bodily motion they make can be life threatening to a human standing around. Even a hiccup can throw a spectator to the ground.

Feeding the bull was especially exciting. It was a chance to sense the immense power and pride of the animal. It was also a time to serve the family economy in a very important way.

I really enjoyed feeding a double handful of grain or hay to Elmer. Elmer happily ate out of my hands. That tongue was about the size of a piece of notebook paper. One swipe cleared the grain from my hand. A second lick wiped my palm smooth.

One summer morning, I tossed some baled alfalfa hay into the rack for Elmer. While I worked, a little puppy, only a few weeks old, played near me. Then that pup made the mistake of his life. He decided those huge legs and long tail would make good teasing material.

The puppy ran into the pen barking and yipping and nipping at the bull's hooves. He could not even cause a little pain to Elmer. Elmer's skin was tough as shoe leather. In fact, it probably became shoe leather, later.

Elmer tried to ignore the pup. He even tried to walk away from the pest. In the process, though, the bull stumbled on the puppy. Elmer pushed it down into the muck of the pen. The pup's head and neck just barely stuck out above the muck.

The puppy could not move. The muck trapped the sad thing. It lay there crying and whining and quivering in fear.

I would have done the same thing. Fear always focuses my actions. I was very much afraid. I was even outside the pen and I was afraid! The pup would die right there unless I pulled it out. Somehow I had to be strong. I had to make something happen.

The rest of the family had gone somewhere and left me home alone to do the chores, and that was all right. At fifteen, being home alone doing the chores is not bad. It is a much more attractive option than a visit to someone's third cousin. Grocery shopping in town would have been even worse. More importantly, I was free of my sisters and my pesky brother for a while.

Truly, I was big enough to handle anything. At least I *thought* I was. As the proud owner of a robin-egg blue 1947 Chevy, the world was mine. That Chevy was a very good car for dating. My younger sisters wanted to ride with me so they could meet boys, and vice versa. A spot at starting left tackle for the high school football team waited for me that year as a sophomore. I could bulldog an 800-pound steer or throw a bale of hay high on a truck.

My body was not the only big and strong part of me. My mind was growing as well. I had read *The Power of Positive Thinking*. The books of Winston Churchill were beginning to replace Zane Grey on the shelf. I had, and still read, a stack of *Life* magazines. They told me all about World War II and Korea.

I knew about Eisenhower, Montgomery, and Patton. Several veterans were close neighbors. They told me about D-Day and Corregidor.

The Bible was a favorite. I especially liked those parts about the underdogs in the fights coming out on top. Spiritually, life was good. Prayer was helping me develop a relationship with God. Powerful prayers are often spoken while working under the business end of a cow. These are not just notions to help pass the time of day. Much developmental conversation with the ultimate power of the universe filtered through my personal history. My mind produced these thoughts while I warded off a dirty cow's tail.

The youth fellowship at church was making an impact on my life. We talked about God and about commitment. Of course, we also talked about girls.

We often struggled with difficult conservation efforts. Our powerful group served advanced ecological interests well. I took fourteen teenagers to the drive-in movie in my car. Dollar night was very good to us, but that's another story. We could take twenty or thirty people to the dollar night show on hay wagons behind a tractor.

We made plans and carried them through. At one meeting we split into teams to plan events. Then we were to come together to vote on which we would do. One team planned a hayride. The other wanted roller skating.

The voting was tied. The girls all voted for roller skating, so we did. Four boys and two girls showed up, out of a group of more than thirty. The two girls were steadies of two of the boys. We had learned well how to plan. Anyway, I knew I was a man.

As a man now, I made plans for that bull. I decided that if I took a pair of pliers and pinched the bull's tail, I would be in control. I had to gain control somehow. If I pinched his tail, the bull would do whatever it was I wanted him to do, or so I thought.

A pair of pliers hung in my pocket, ready. They helped me cut the wires on the hay bales. I quickly stepped into the pen to take control of the situation. Elmer was still just standing there, looking down at the squealing pup, puzzled. No time to waste. It was my time to act.

Wouldn't you know it? Those pliers would not open far enough to get a grip on the bull's tail. I had this sudden vision of Popeye inflating his muscles. All I could do was pull a few hairs from that big tail. It was nothing but muscle and bone.

One of my cousins had told me I could twist the bull's tail. This would have the same effect as using the pliers. I grabbed that tail and twisted. It would fit neatly into a "wrong-end half-nelson." Sure it would; it was about the same thickness as my thigh and ten times as strong. I tried to shove Elmer away from the pup, using tail twisting as the persuader.

Elmer turned and looked at me with the big question. "What in the world are you trying to do back there, anyway?"

FFlloooppp! Suddenly, that tail was telephone-pole straight. Elmer started beating me alongside the head as if he were Ted Williams in batting practice.

I grabbed the tail again and twisted some more. Then I pushed and shoved harder to get that bull to move. I was in deep trouble again, and deep in other stuff, too. Sure, I had a hammerlock on the bull's tail, and I was even steadily moving the bull away from the pup. He moved over one inch at a time.

Have you ever had a feeling that things were bad, and going to get worse — quickly? That something — not really pleasant — was about to happen? Well....

My parents and teachers always made a point of saying, "Don't just sit there, make something happen. Move it, buster. Make decisions. Choose which one to serve, but choose and serve!"

For most of us, I think, that is not easy. The risks are great. We might fail the chosen path utterly. We might choose the wrong service. The worst suffering for most of us is to think of dying alone and unnoticed, thinking, "Who would miss me at the end?" Calloused hands seem a necessity for the comfort of a dying man.

In that bullpen, that day, I was making something happen. It felt good. I was the kingpin. Hero, even! Even with the ramrod-straight tail on the bull, I was still in charge. I was making something happen. Yeah!

Then he surprised me. That bull started rocking sideways. He was moving over a bit with each swing. Good! Something was going to give!

No one said it would be me that gave. Rocking Elmer shifted his weight again. He began to move his hind end right and left, left and right. I tried to help him with my shoulder when he rocked away from the pup.

Keeping up with all that swinging ton of bull was not easy in the deep muck. With every swing the bull moved me farther out on the pendulum. At first, I had trouble pulling my feet out of the mire fast enough. I tried to keep up by hanging on Elmer's tail. Soon, however, that wasn't the problem.

Better planning would probably have helped. That is often the case. Perhaps another lesson or two from the youth group would have simplified my life. Maybe I should have listened carefully to another good sermon.

Frustration was setting in pretty fast. Even God might not be working to help me with my frustration. Clearly, God did not have an interest in helping me with that ton of bull.

My frustration with God grew. Couldn't God see what was going on? Why would God not help me? I was doing what God called me to do! Doesn't Elmer know I am a Christian? By now he was slamming me against the corral poles with the wildest swings. Elmer was much more violent than my sisters — he could clobber me with his little dance.

All sense of social justice or theological perspective was gone. Even the puppy was not particularly important to my well-being any longer. Survival seemed suddenly critical. Forget social and creational justice, I had to get out of there!

That thought made the hero in me begin to storm at my over-sized adversary. My soul raged at the thought of giving up. This was only one of God's lower creatures. I could think of nothing worse than giving up to a simple animal. The poor pup would die right there in the muck of the bullpen if I quit. God was calling me to do something stupendously righteous and powerful.

Anger came now from deep inside me. This stupid bull just had to do my will. He had before. A year earlier Elmer the Holstein broke out of his pen while our parents were gone for a livestock show. He went to the neighbors for a visit. While there, he had fun with a couple of their registered purebred Jersey heifers. Leading him home was my job. That is another story.

This bull was going to be mine. I was in charge. No one else was close. I would have appreciated some help, of course, but I knew I must press on alone! Elmer and I were having some difficulty with each other. One cannot go for help while holding on to a bull's tail with both hands. The only movement I could handle was to avoid slamming against the corral poles repeatedly.

Bang! By now my head was starting to go numb. My sisters and teachers said it had been that way for some time, but this was different. My muscles hurt as if they were going to let go at any moment.

Bang! The fence, again. One boot came off in the muck. It felt as if my pants would come off as well. This was not a convenient time to check. Besides, even if they were dropping, that was just tough. Taking the time to refasten the belt seemed inappropriate just then. I could not grip the tail with both hands and pull my pants up at the same time. Priorities, perhaps. If the neighbors did not want to watch, they should turn away.

Bang! Someone had to take charge to make something happen. Enough of this stalling and monkeying around. This dangerous situation had to change, and it had to change quickly. What to do? The bull was in my kingdom, so I had to think of something.

My mind's eye pictured all the tools and weapons that were just out of reach. The pitchforks, the hayhooks, the rope. There might not be much value trying to reason with Elmer. I could never win an argument with him or my father, anyway.

The bull gave me a few more slams against the fence. Then a really courageous, simple, and stupid idea came to me. The simplicity of it was startling. It might have been the only doable action, but it was also the only plan my nimble and aching brain could hatch.

The circumstances called for brave action. Nothing less would suffice for my own ego or for the survival of the puppy. I faced the "put up or shut up" time for a would-be action figure hero.

The bull moved me again toward the wall for another slam. My feet came very close to the whimpering puppy. As the bull bullied me into the poles, I let go and reached for the pup. Risky — oh, so risky! I could have fallen head first in the muck! Or Elmer could have stepped on me!

I grabbed a double handful of slop along with the poor little pup. Holding it as gently as possible, I tried to jump toward the gate, a few feet away. With my foot stuck in the slop, jumping was impossible. With a second motion, I threw the pup and the slop under the bottom log of the fence. With the same motion, I tried to get to the gate, but didn't quite make it. Elmer swung his rump toward me again as I stood up. This threw me toward the fence. My head banged hard on the solid latch post.

Consciousness returned some time later. I was lying on the ground directly under a corral pole. My head faced Elmer, standing close now to watch. The thought of Elmer stepping on my face panicked me, but I need not have worried.

My head was throbbing from hitting the gate pole. The corral logs were not soft, except where I had repeatedly hit them. It took some time to clear the cobwebs. Only then did I realize my heart was still beating.

Gathering myself, I slowly became aware of one of the most horrible stenches any human had ever known. With terrible fear I opened one eye and looked straight up the cavernous nostrils of the biggest face imaginable. They were large enough to hold a big teenage fist in each nostril, with enough room to bend an elbow. I figured I could scratch his ears from inside.

Just then a bath-towel size tongue spread itself over my face. It felt like soggy sandpaper. It was a precious gift from a gentle giant. His kind gift softly healed the cuts and scratches and bumps and bruises on my face.

I lived, the puppy lived, and I got my boot back. Somehow the pup never smelled the same again. Maybe I didn't, either. I finally retrieved my boot from the muck, but it never changed its scent, before or after.

Some critters bow to their place in creation in the strangest ways.

When God calls you to action, be prepared for that sandpaper tongue.

59

What Is It To Be Human?

Synopsis: The death of an infant brings the basic question for humanity to a small community in Nebraska.

Liturgical Calendar: Lent 4, Cycle B; any memorial, funeral, or recognition of dementia

Scriptures: Numbers 21:4-9; Psalm 107:1-3, 17-22; Ephesians 2:1-10; John 3:14-21

Comment: A true story.

The new grandmother called me early in the morning. This was one of the many times in my career I have heard tears falling. Her very tired voice brought me to a moment of my own sadness for her and her family.

Her daughter-in-law had given birth in the night. The delivery was by caesarean section. Things had not gone well at any time.

The pregnancy was not a comfortable process. The young mother spent a lot of time trying to bring this child to full term. She spent time in the hospital and made many visits to the obstetrician in efforts to deliver a healthy baby. We were all afraid this was not to be.

The infant finally came. She was severely deformed, inside and out. Her most serious problem lay in the construction of her heart.

In an effort to help the baby and save her life, the medical team flew her to Denver for care. We all knew there was little chance to save her, but everyone felt it was necessary. She needed her own chance to live.

She lived only three or four days. Everyone tried their best to help her, but all the efforts together were not enough. The family asked me to do a memorial service in the church. They were life-long members of the small congregation. The family already felt the love and support of their friends and neighbors. The little family group needed to be together in this sadness.

At the time set for the service, the sanctuary was completely full. The organist played a few favorite hymns. Someone sang some songs of faith. At various points, between the songs, I read Psalm 23 and some favorites from the gospel of Luke. I read Luke 18:15-17 and 20:20-21, then 1 John 4:7-12 and Revelation 21:1-4.

A memorial for an infant can be quite difficult for the pastor as well as for the family. In a half-century of professional ministry, I have found only one message that seems satisfactory and that message is this:

"Dearly beloved, you and I come here today torn by the death of Janey. Janey barely seems to have had enough life to mention. She did not live long enough to write a book, or even sign her name. She will never have a child who will be a great athlete or movie star.

"Janey will never know what it is to get a good grade, or even a failing grade in school. She will never drive a car. She did fly in an airplane, but I suspect she did not realize what was happening.

"Janey will never hold a lover's hand in marriage. She will never wear a pretty necklace, or a bright apron. She will never share a secret with her mother or her father or her older sister.

"Does this mean that all is lost? Does all this mean that Janey will never have a life? Has her mother's struggle to keep her alive been a waste? Will her father have worked those countless hours to provide her with a home and medical care and toys and clothing for no return? Have the grandparents prayed and lifted and supported the family for naught?

"Of course not! All these things have purpose and a value of their own. All these things are part of human life. The measure of life is in how we are loved, not in how much we can love another.

"There is one who loves us dearly, and shows it. God, our Creator, is the great lover for us. A child such as Janey must be reckoned as having lived a full life. The reason is simple. She has been loved, is loved, and will be loved.

"Janey has been loved, is loved, and will be loved by God. I have very little to say beyond this about God's love. It is eternal,

61

steadfast, completely willing to risk everything for Janey. God is even willing to die on the cross for Janey and for you and for me. God will do anything for Janey and for you and for me.

"Janey has been loved, is loved, and will be loved by her parents and grandparents. The death of a child cannot kill the love between a parent and a child. This is part of Jesus' message about being born again. We cannot re-enter the womb and pretend we were never born. Something about pregnancy and childbirth solidifies the love between parent and child. We do not always understand it, but it is there.

"Janey has been loved, is loved, and will be loved by the community. You, friends and neighbors, cousins and aunts and uncles. I know that any of you would have sacrificed yourself for Janey if it had been needed. We would have done that because she lived. It is not because she was friendly, or had a soft touch, or pretty eyes. We love because we know we are loved by God and by one another.

"My friends, this is the source of being human. It is the power that means more than anything else to us. We are loved by God, our Creator. We are loved by Christ, the one who walks and talks with us. God loves us. Therefore, we are human. Our lives are complete. It is only as God loves us that we are fully human.

"Then, of course, it becomes our task to love others. We do not love others just because someone has told us to do it. We love one another because God first loves us. We do whatever we can to make life good for one another as a response to God's love.

"We want to respond properly to God's love for us. 'Beloved, let us love one another. Everyone who loves is born of God, and loves God' (1 John 4:7). That is our response.

"We can answer the question of whether Janey had a complete and full life. She did. She does. She has been loved by God, by her family, and by us. She *is* loved by God, by her family, and by us. Janey *will be loved* by God, by her family, and by us. That is enough."

Following the message we sang a simple children's song and went home.

I Am Alone

Synopsis: An elderly man in a skilled care nursing center pleads for attention.

Liturgical Calendar: Lent 3, Cycle C

Scriptures: Isaiah 55:1-9; Psalm 63:1-8; 1 Corinthians 10:1-13; Luke 13:1-9

Comment: A true story. How do we show love?

I visited an elderly man in an elderly care facility in Cottage Grove, Oregon. While I sat beside him, for about ten minutes, he gave me these words about himself.

"I am alone. Sounds in the dark terrify me. No one comes to me to whisper to me that everything is all right. No one dries my tears.

"I am alone. I fear for my sanity. No one reasons with me, or argues with me, or questions life with me. No one tells me I am wrong.

"I am alone. I forget how to talk because no one talks to me. I forget how to listen.

"I am alone. I do not know what is important to me or to anyone else. I have no goals, no dreams, and no future. Who would know if a good thing happened to me?

"I am alone. I do not count the days anymore. No one shares time with me. I cannot even tear the pages from the calendar to give to someone else.

"I am alone. My emotions die for lack of water. I have no relationship, no touch of hearts to build with tears of sadness or laughter.

"I am alone. I have no love. No one else is here for me to love.

"May I love you?"

The Innkeeper

Synopsis: An innkeeper struggles to earn a living in very difficult circumstances. A contemporary version of the most wonderful birth.

Liturgical Calendar: Christmas 1, Cycle B

Scriptures: Isaiah 61:10—62:3; Psalm 148; Galatians 4:4-7; Luke 2:22-40

Comment: This story should help people take the reality of the birth of Christ into their own lives.

Letter to the Editor:

When are we going to stand up for our rights as free citizens? I am sick and tired of this riffraff. They come into town day after day, week after week, and make a mess. I run a small motel on the main street. These people are just destroying me.

They take over our streets. A bunch of bedouin camel jockeys could not be worse. They frighten our children and our old people. They throw rocks at our dogs and steal our sheep and goats to eat.

And dirty — good grief — one would think they never learned to bathe. It is too much even to walk on the same side of the street with some of them. They are just so filthy. I can't even hire someone to clean their rooms when they finally leave.

They cram so many people into a room it is not funny. They pay for two people and sneak ten or fifteen more into the room. We call the police, but the dispatcher says they don't have enough officers on duty to do anything.

We need to build a fence around the town to keep these people out. Then we can have peace for ourselves.

Now, they have gone too far. Last night a couple came to the motel wanting a room. I didn't have one available, not even one that had not been cleaned. I did want to help them.

These two looked and seemed like decent people. Mind you, I am not prejudiced. I just like people to respect me and my possessions. The woman was very young and very pregnant — *very* pregnant.

The husband — I guess he was her husband — begged for some place to shelter her. Finally, I let them to go to the storage barn for the night. The barn has no bathroom, but at least they could stay warm and dry. This was the kind thing to do, anyway.

I told them no smoking. Too much dry straw and hay lay around out there to allow smoking.

Well, what a night! The couple had not been out there more than a couple hours when one of the local children came in to say that some woman had a baby out there. For crying out loud!

Oh, well, I guess I could feel sorry for them and let that go. I was not charging them for the place to sleep, and already they were adding more people!

Just after midnight, it seemed that these two had moved in half the town. Goodness knows how much money we lost on those free roomers. All manner of people started coming — sheepherders (probably to buy pot, I suppose) and rich people. Even some people I could not sort started coming. They seemed to come for some kind of costume party.

Someone started a fire. A bright light shined out through the door. The fire department should have come for an illegal burn. I did not call them. It probably would have meant a ticket for me.

By this time, I was scared. I called the police again. The dispatcher gave me the same song and dance about "not enough officers." No way would I go out there by myself. No other Galileans would go out there with me.

So I just chose to survive. I just let them have the place. That's all I could do. I stayed inside, afraid even to go out to my own barn. I was afraid what might happen to me if I walked down my own path.

Fortunately, by morning the sheepherders and their pals were gone. I guess all the drugs were gone, as well. The bums have not come back.

I politely asked the father to please not have his friends back again tonight. He just smiled and said, "Okay."

No concern. No big deal. I think they left just after that. I bet they did not go straight home. They probably went to Egypt or something.

That is enough! If the government wants to collect taxes, raise them. They can spend some taxes paying for the damage people like this do to our businesses. To make us pay is like taxation without representation.

Now to top it all, some military intelligence people were just here. They said some big shot had died. These trench-coat people were looking for a certain baby boy — to be the new king, I overheard. The government is not going to help pay the rent for those people. Probably we can show it as business damage on the tax form. I refuse to help the government find its own king when I cannot pay my own bills.

I really don't think that family out in the barn could produce a worthwhile leader, anyway.

It makes me boil to see where our society is headed.

Sincerely,
Yosef bar Mikal

Kava

Synopsis: A Tongan couple must sacrifice their daughter to obey the law of the land.

Liturgical Calendar: Epiphany

Scriptures: Exodus 17:1-7; Psalm 95; Romans 5:1-11; John 4:5-42; 1 John 4:7-21

Comment: A traditional story. This is one of many versions of this story I have heard. Ethnic Tongans celebrate the Kava Feast or Kava Circle widely around the world. This story is the basis for these circles.

The traditional Kava Circle asks the group to sit cross-legged on the ground. A kava root tea in coconut half-shells is the group's sacramental element. The leader or another person tells the story of the girl, Kava. The participants are usually free to speak of anything they wish, including their own lives. *Tevita* is the Polynesian translation of "David." This word is used around the world as "The Great One," or "The Leader."

Once upon a time, there lived a man and his wife on a far inhabitable island of Tonga. The island was Eueiki. Fevanga and Fefafa had grown up together. In their early teens, they were married to each other by their families. This was the custom in those days.

Fevanga and Fefafa devoted themselves to each other. Although it seemed they were unable to have children, they never quit trying. They never placed any blame on the other for their infertility.

As Fevanga and Fefafa were growing older, still without children, they prayed desperately to God for a child. Theirs was the despair of the ages. No child would survive them to carry on the family living.

Every day they cried out their prayers for a child. Finally, God heard their cries. At long last a child was born. Fevanga and Fefafa named their gift of love Kava.

Kava was not a well child. The girl who was the pleasure and treasure of Fevanga and Fefafa had a skin condition that was not good. It sometimes made her unattractive to look at. Sometimes patches of her skin became rough and scaly. She could not eat well, nor was she strong in her play. Both parents had to spend much time tending her and feeding her.

From the day she was born, at least one parent had to be with her always. Sometimes, Fefafa stayed up all night to be certain Kava slept well. Sometimes, Fevanga took his turn all night so Fefafa and Kava could rest together.

Sometimes, Fefafa only dreamed she had eaten a meal, she was so tired. Kava grew toward being a woman. She was truly the jewel of her parents, even with her hard skin.

Because the three of them were the only people to live on the island, few people knew about the girl. Only the tax man who came around each year was aware of the little family on Eueiki. He came to collect the coconuts and pearls that paid the taxes to King Tevita.

Besides him, only those who might have looked at the tax records might have known. No other person cared.

The family was very poor. They ate only what they could get from the sea and from the few coconut trees on the island. They survived. Sometimes they were very hungry.

The girl was growing and becoming very beautiful in her spirit. She was very smart. She was also very nice to her parents.

It was royal Tongan duty for the king to visit each inhabited island during his reign. One day, King Tevita announced his desire to see this little bit of rock and sand. When he checked the records, he learned of a small family there.

He sent word that he would come to the island in a few days. He would come in his big canoe, with ten men paddling. Other canoes would carry his guards and his servants, with food for the servants.

This was a very difficult time for Fevanga and Fefafa. They knew the law *required* them to prepare a meal for the king and his attendants. This was a tax from the king and his counselors.

The big day came. King Tevita arrived in his royal dugout canoe with many others. In the royal canoe, five men paddled on each side in smooth rhythm. As they worked, they sang songs recounting the great history of King Tevita's father.

At last, King Tevita landed on the tiny island home of the family. Fevanga and Fefafa treated King Tevita to all they could make for the occasion. King Tevita was very pleased.

The king went across the island, inspecting what little there was. He told Fevanga and Fefafa that he was very proud of them. He said they were very good people for Tonga.

After the king left the island, a few bits of food were left. Fevanga and Fefafa found a nice spot on the island and buried the remaining food carefully.

When the king left the island he traveled back toward the main island. While on the canoe, the king asked someone where the girl was. His tax records showed she lived on the island. No one could say where she was.

When the king arrived back at his palace, he became very ill. His head hurt with the pain known as the Crown of Thorns. His mouth was unable to open and to swallow. Everyone thought he would die.

The king sent the nobleman Lo'au back to the island to learn why Fevanga and Fefafa had poisoned the king. Lo'au went with many warriors to talk with Fevanga and Fefafa.

When Lo'au came to the island, Fevanga and Fefafa told him that they were very poor. They told him that the only food they had to offer the king was Kava, their daughter.

When Lo'au returned, he told the king what had happened. This news brought great sadness to King Tevita. For an entire week, the king mourned the little girl. Through his tears, King Tevita searched for some way to rebuild the lives of Fevanga and Fefafa. He also wanted to recover from the evil of his own position. King Tevita knew his demand for food had placed an unbearable burden on Fevanga and Fefafa. His pain was of his own making. In deep sadness, the king sent Lo'au back to the island to ask forgiveness.

When Lo'au came to the island, he told Fevanga and Fefafa of the illness and the sadness of King Tevita. They took Lo'au to the spot that held the last bit of Kava. He saw a tree growing over her grave. Lo'au placed a blessing on the tree. Now this tree would provide food for Fevanga and Fefafa for the rest of their lives. When Lo'au was on the island, he told Fevanga and Fefafa to prepare one shell of root tea. This tea, given to a stranger each year, would pay the royal tax.

The next year, the tree was full-grown and filled with flowers. In full time it provided fruit for the family. When the king came again to visit, Fefafa dried some roots of the tree. She used a stone bowl to grind them into a powder. She mixed the powder with water and gave the drink to the king.

When the king drank the liquid, his mouth and his head began to feel better at once. He sat with his advisors and began to plan the affairs of Tonga. For the first time in a year, his head did not hurt.

One matter the king decided to deal with was the hunger of his people on the islands. The king, himself, went back to the little island home of Fevanga and Fefafa.

The king invited Fevanga and Fefafa to sit on the ground with him. The royal council sat, too. Together they drank the liquid made from the root of the tree. Fevanga stirred the drink while Fefafa served the king in half a coconut shell.

As the three of them talked together, they talked of all the matters of Tonga. They talked of the beautiful Kava. They talked as friend to friend, not as king to subject.

Finally, the pain of the memory of Kava was gone. All that remained was the aura of her beauty and love. The commitment of Fevanga and Fefafa to Tonga and the king replaced the sadness.

The king decided to make a magic tree from the seeds. He told his people to plant them on every island of Tonga. No matter how poor a family might be, they would have some food when the king came to visit. When the king went to visit, all sat around in a circle to drink the kava drink. The group passed the kava tea around the circle in a half coconut shell. Each drank a few sips and passed the shell on to another. There was laughing and joking. Many retold old stories. They made decisions that were important to the family and community.

It was very good. All those who took the kava slept well that night.

Kick The Can

Synopsis: Heroes must choose their responses carefully. Community fun night brings a lesson in responsible timing.

Liturgical Calendar: Proper 9, Ordinary Time 14, Cycle A

Scriptures: Genesis 24:34-67; Psalm 45:10-17; Romans 6:12-23; Matthew 11:28-30

Comment: A true story. Every leader and hero has obstacles to tackle.

"Kick The Can" was a favorite sport in Nu Acres. Those long summer evenings were just right before we had television in our neighborhood. Time flew by while we hid. Occasionally, one found a minute or two for some mild pleasantry while hiding with a favorite partner. Of course, one should be prepared to run for the base at any moment. What the heck! Seize the girl! — seize the moment!

It did not last long enough. I finally saw why the older children always wanted to hide in pairs. The trouble was that television finally did arrive. That box changed the whole thing.

Our farm had some old machinery scattered around out behind the barn. Every inch of all that stuff was as well known to me as my feet. It should be. I barked my shins on it every time I went into the area after dark. Finding the cows or the pigs or a forgotten baseball could be very painful.

One cozy evening, I had stayed hidden a very long time. As a baseball announcer would say, "I bin hid a ton." Baseball players and television announcers limit themselves to words of three letters or less. For the same reason, baseball uses only four bases. Announcers probably cannot handle more.

Back to my hiding place. I was there a long time. Because it was some distance away from the base, my position was secure. I could just relax and grin.

Well, sort of relax and grin. I hid in the box of an old potato planter. The job of the planter was to open a trench in the ground. Then it dropped chunks of potato into the trench. The planter had a large wheel with a series of needles on it. These needles each grabbed a piece of potato and dropped it into the little trench.

This sounds great, normally. However, this was not a normal time. A needle that poked into the seed potatoes had found another target. My posterior was becoming most uncomfortable. Tetanus was a real risk.

Laughing and screaming came from the direction of the base. I was cool. I just waited for my heroic moment. The critical time was coming, and quickly. If any aspired to be the neighborhood hero, they should be ready now.

Perhaps we should review the international rules of Kick The Can. The *Nu Acres Gnus* prints the rules. One person is "It." All the rest go hide. It counts to some insignificant number such as 100 or 63. Then It goes on to search for the rest. Upon finding a suspect, It runs to the base, slaps the base, counts "one, two, three," and calls the name of the person.

If, however, the "findee" runs faster and gets to the can first (honestly, it really is a can), things change. The findee kicks it and shouts "go free" before It gets to base. Then everyone who has been caught runs to hide again. When everyone is together in the pen together, the round is over. The first person caught by It is It for the next go-round.

I waited and waited. Knowing how to wait coolly is critical for success. Then I waited a bit longer. My heart overflowed with the good feelings and appreciation of all those who were in the pen.

Me! The hero! I could run in, kick the can, cry "go free," and release the whole bunch. I could even come back here to hide again. No one had found me. My hiding place was secure. I would be the most loved person in the world that night. Well, at least in Nu Acres. I might even get some choice partner to hide with me. In a different hiding place, of course.

It was time to make my move. Very cagily and quietly, I left my post, the seed potato bin. Because my body was so cramped from the long stay in the bin of the planter my legs were jammed.

Moving them was rather painful for a moment. Crawling under the electric fence was the only way. Those spry, young legs could not jump the fence as they normally did.

I snuck around the haystack, still watching carefully for It. He must be nearing frustrated exhaustion by now. He could not cease from looking for me around the garage, behind the car, and past the rosebush. He would be looking past the old one-holer we used for emergencies such as power outages or family reunions.

In the driveway, in all its glory, stood "the can." This treasure was just an old Folger's can. It had been bent and straightened too often. The can sat out there in the middle of the driveway. It just begged someone — me, namely — to give it a swift kick. I could not see the captives yet. They were all sitting on the porch out of my line of sight. They must be groaning to be free. They must be moaning about their unfortunate circumstances.

I ran. Oh, how I ran, as fast as fast can be. I put every bit of energy I had into that last dash for community freedom. As the can flew off into the darkness, I cried, "Go free! Go free!" Then I listened for the shouts of liberty from the captives. Turning to face them in the dim light, I would now proudly receive their heartfelt thanks and cheers.

There was silence — absolute silence. I looked again. Nobody was there — absolutely nobody. No one was on the porch. No one was under the tree. The driveway was empty.

Then I heard the murmur of voices from inside the house. Surely they were not hiding in there!

No, they were not hiding. The group stood around or sat out in the open of the living room and the kitchen. They were in plain sight of God and everyone. The group felt no fear. No anxiety panicked them. No yearning for freedom was openly expressed.

The game had finished fifteen minutes earlier when the ice cream freezer finally quit. By the time this forgotten worldly hero came around, the ice cream was gone.

They had even played another full round of Kick The Can!

No one knew the difference.

She's Still There

Synopsis: The Copper Lady of New York Harbor is still a beacon to freedom.

Liturgical Calendar: Proper 8, Ordinary Time 13, Cycle C

Scriptures: 2 Kings 2:1-2, 11-20; Psalm 77:1-2, 11-20; Galatians 5:1, 13-25; Luke 9:51-62

Comment: A true story. A visit to the Statue of Liberty in New York City harbor is one of the most significant pilgrimages any person can make.

There's something about America,
    She stands to speak.

Oh, she's still there.
    I looked.

Someone said the Grand Old Lady had been
    destroyed
    torn apart
    shattered
    ... and forgotten.
        But I don't know ...

She's still there,
    flame held high,
    crying into the night

"Give them all,
    carry to my shore, to my arms."

Some say there's no more room,
    the prairies are full,
    the cities are running over.
      NO MORE ROOM!
        But I don't know ...

She's still there,
    copper skin turned green,
    concrete base worn smooth,
    power of the franc worn thin.

Some say there's no more room for
    copper and concrete,
    steel and stone,
    macadam and muscle.
      But I don't know ...

She's still there,
    ferries of tourists,
    pockets of travelers' checks
      managers
        plumbers
          baseball players ...

I've got mine!
  and
      That's enough!
      No more!

      But I don't know ...

She's still there,
    millions staring through the crown,
    eyes a-peer to share the scene
      of Cubans
        of Haitians
          of Laotians

and Pakistanis ...
my people, all ...

come to pack into our streets
come to study in our schools
come to compete with us for jobs.

Some say replace the flame
with sign of eight sides painted red:
Stop
Taking
Our
Places!
But I don't know ...

She's still there,
flame alit with beck'ning power
taking naught from me but love
which cast about returns,
making me a model more
of God's intent to be.
She's still there,
working magic for struggling masses,
bringing name, perhaps, or fame,
or riches more?
Or is it "Vote for Me,
The Proven One?"

Whatever 'tis,
'tis Liberty!
And this I know ...

She's still there.
I looked,
I cried,

She welcomed me with open arms.
　　May she always be as she is today.

She's still there.
　　For me.
　　　　For you.
　　　　　　For heroes proved
　　　　　　　　and Liberty.

Lonny

Synopsis: A small-town boy, Lonny, searches for the big life on Manhattan. Lonny finds new relationship with his parents.

Liturgical Calendar: Proper 22, Ordinary Time 27, Cycle C

Scriptures: Lamentations 1:1-6; Psalm 137; 2 Timothy 1:1-14; Luke 17:5-10

Comment: A common occurrence in our world.

Once upon a time, in a small American town there lived a typical small family: husband, wife, and son. The father, Jerry, was a reasonably successful businessman, owner and operator of "Jerry's Auto Parts." The mother, Luann, was a part-time homemaker and part-time accountant for Jerry's Auto Parts.

Jerry and Luann had a good life. They did many things that most of us dream of doing. They had built a new home. Sometimes they made a pilgrimage to some interesting place in the world. They put their son, Lonny, through college.

It was the dream of Jerry and Luann that, after college, Lonny would return to run the family business. They would call it "L-J-L Auto Parts." Perhaps with Lonny's know-how they could expand. Three or four stores in neighboring towns would be about right. The three of them working together could handle them well. The unity of the family working and dreaming together looked like the all-American family future.

We might guess that Lonny had some other things he wanted to do first. After graduation, Lonny packed. He put a couple pairs of pants, a couple of shirts, and an old *National Geographic* map in an old backpack. On the back of a JC Penney's charge statement he wrote his parents a quick note. Silently, Lonny slipped out of the house in the dark of night, and hit the road.

Two places seem to appeal to young people, to young wanderers of all ages in America. These havens beckon one to seek fame and fortune. These are meccas with a constant supply of uncharted roads. Instant success is a possibility here. Here we fulfill our dreams easily. This make-believe world has a western center in the Los Angeles basin — Disneyland, Hollywood and Vine, UCLA, United Artists, and the rest of California. The other center of this strange world is much farther east.

Lonny stepped out of the house into the cool summer night. It took half an hour of walking to get to the interstate. In a few minutes more he stood beneath a red, white, and blue shield lit by the light of a tall, aluminum torch. The shield clearly stated that this was Eastbound Interstate 80.

Lonny wasn't your average dummy. He hadn't come to New York to be a failure. A good education, successful and stable parents, and good personal habits made landing a good job likely.

Lonny left his last ride near the Port Authority Building. His first purchase in New York was well planned. It was not cocaine peddled by the spindly legged street vendors. He ignored their half-whispered sing-sing, "Coke, need a little coke? Fix you up with a little coke, make you feel good all over...."

Nor was it even a hot dog or a pretzel from street peddlers. These merchants of quick foods spent their days and nights searching for that perfect location. Every new spot might be where each following day would be a sell-out. They could not entice Lonny.

No, Lonny was smarter than all that. His first purchase was a *Wall Street Journal*. He quickly opened it to the "Help Wanted" section. Page after page of potential careers — and surely one of those prestigious careers was just right for him. With some more of his precious hoard of graduation money he bought a suit. It was not a flashy suit. It was one just right for office work. It could double for mixing and mingling with the upper crust of his slice of Big Apple pie.

The first week brought frustration and disappointment. The next week brought the bitterness of being told he was too young or too inexperienced. Then came anger at being told he was not familiar with the city or that he took the wrong courses in college. Sometimes it seemed he was the wrong religion. Lonny began to change. He no longer bought the *Wall Street Journal*, but the *Times*. Clerks saw him regularly at the employment offices.

The rejections began to change. No longer was he underqualified, he was overqualified. He had too much education to check groceries for the A&P. Mo laughed at him when he applied to wash dishes at "Mo's Lunches."

With his money running out, the new college graduate moved from his room. Lonny began sleeping in doorways or under the bridges in town. He began to sell off whatever he had. Everything went but his backpack, his home away from home.

In pure humiliation, Lonny tossed between his need to eat and his attachment to his backpack. He argued with himself to the point of numbness. With a last gasp of hope, Lonny approached another young man who had given up and was going home. A deal was struck, a backpack for a guitar.

Lonny began to sing. At first, few people paid any attention to one more voice on the night-filled streets of Manhattan. The coins seldom clinked in the coffee can on the "Oranges from Florida" box. They rarely dropped, but Lonny ate, and he kept singing. His songs were songs of desperation and loneliness, of frustration and hurt.

It had been a long time since Lonny had written his parents. Too long. With a sense of shame, every letter written began and ended the same way: "Dear Mom and Dad...." They never went any further.

Each time Lonny wanted to write home, one of the psalms came out of his memory and stood beside him. For hours, the crowds in front of him took on strange shapes and forms. They seemed faceless and nameless to Lonny. He let his mind fog itself in an old psalm. Lonny remembered another time and place and people, much like this one.

> *By the rivers of Babylon —*
> *There we sat down and there we wept*
> *when we remembered Zion.*
> *On the willows there we hung up our harps.*
> *For there our captors asked us for songs,*

and our tormentors asked for mirth, saying,
"Sing us one of the songs of Zion!"
How could we sing the Lord's song in a foreign land?
If I forget you, O Jerusalem,
let my right hand wither!
Let my tongue cling to the roof of my mouth
if I do not remember you,
if I do not set Jerusalem above my highest joy.
— Psalm 137:1-6 (NRSV)

Lonny began to hate. He began to hate the demons that held him prisoner every night at 38th and Broadway. He began to hate the system that held him apart from success — and from home.

The system had lied to him. The system had said that success was right around the corner. "Take your degree and claim your place in the world!" Lonny had gone right around the corner to the city called the greatest city in the world. He must claim his place. Now he had claimed his place and was surely starving to death both in body and in spirit.

Nights of cold hunger crawled through his body and ate into his bones, trailing isolation and despair. The rest of Psalm 137 came into his mind. It only added to his hurt and frustration:

O daughter Babylon, you devastator!
Happy shall be the one who pays you back
what you have done to us!
Happy shall they be who take your little ones
and dash them against the rock!
— Psalm 137:8-9 (NRSV)

One night, as those words were bringing tears to Lonny's eyes, he felt lost. Forms and faces in front were being lost to darkness and confusion and red eyes. Lonny became aware of a strange movement in the crowd — a silence, a shuffle, a tension.

Lonny forced his eyes into a half-focus now. He began to make out the form of someone picking up the empty coffee can from the box. Then moving along the face of the small crowd, the form began silently urging coins and paper into it. Lonny only sang until

81

the form came again, placing the now half-full can on the box in front of Lonny. Then the form moved off into the darkness. The outline of a familiar face in the glow of taxi headlights told Lonny his father was in town.

The next night, Lonny was back at his same place singing mechanically. He paid no heed to the press of unformed faces around him. Lonny waited and sang for someone to put some money in the can. Jerry, having seen the low estate of his only son, would go back to the store and leave Lonny alone. Jerry would go home with his shame and his hurt, and nothing could be done about it.

Late in the evening the crowds began to come out of the theaters, from *Annie* and *Elephant Man*. They were escaping the assault of the open immorality of the Great White Way. While they streamed past, the form was back. The silent father again picked up the empty coffee can and began passing it among the crowd.

He stood with tears streaming down his silent face, watching and listening as Lonny sang. Then he was gone.

Lonny sang alone, unaware that the crowds had long gone. Thoughts far from the songs blurred his vision. "Why, oh why, did he have to come and see me like this? Why did he have to share my shame? Now I can never go home, or even write home."

Slowly, Lonny emptied the contents of his coffee can into his pocket. He began to walk with a new purpose. He did not run with fear or anger. His embarrassment in front of his father drove him on through the streets. Several hours later, the lights of the street dimmed and faded in the morning sun. In the dawn, Lonny walked down Broadway with no mind for the empty shops and theaters. He had no awareness of the early sun cascading off the World Trade Center.

He had to find a new location, a new home. He would search out a place where the owner of Jerry's Auto Parts would not think to look for him. Somewhere he would find a haven from the sad eyes of his father.

He bought a ticket with the money from the can. When the ferry started running, he caught the first ferry out to the Copper Lady, the Mother of Freedom. With rich tourists from Japan and Germany and Kansas and Los Angeles, this ought to be good. There ought to be money here, and success. Discovery and fame and prestige should be Lonny's.

Best of all, no one would suspect who he was or where his home had been. On the walkway, just off the ferry, before the broad concrete steps of the statue Lonny began to sing and play.

A fierce determination for independence and success came over Lonny. He now sang his songs with a fierce determination. His voice had been only mechanical the night before as he hurled them into the air on Broadway. He would become a great singer, a great entertainer, a power in the musical world. Jerry should be a proud father. Maybe even one day someone would write the story of Lonny's life! There would be no more sad eyes.

With terror in his heart, Lonny knew he was found. An arm, a familiar arm, had him by the waist — not grasping or clawing, just a father holding his son. Without looking, Lonny could see those sad eyes and the now three-day-old stubble of a beard.

Still without looking, he felt himself turning and holding and crying softly on the quivering shoulder. Then the shoulder was gone. Lonny was alone again.

Just as quickly as Jerry had come out of his home and out of the racks of auto parts, he was gone.

That night, the crowds again streamed out of their confrontations with Oliver Warbucks and David Merrick. The tourists mixed with hot dog vendors and leathercrafters. Lonny again sang on the corner. As he sang, thinking of his father, he began to wonder if his dad would be back that night. Lonny began to look carefully at the faces, hoping he might see that familiar face. He had to look at faces.

Lonny recognized the clothes, though not the faces. He remembered the girl who wore eleven dresses at once. The man who clapped his hands to silk trousers with the beat of Lonny's tunes. Even the smells of the people were familiar — the garlic and pretzels. One that needed a bath.

As he looked for his father's face he saw other faces around him for the first time. Lonny began to smile. They were faces with noses and eyes and ears and whiskers and lipstick. Lonny sang with joy.

83

He sang timidly at first. Soon the tears of joy and freedom spread over his soul. Then the moment of release and embrace on the steps of the Statue of Release came back to overwhelm him. He looked up through tears of joy, seeing faces — open, accepting, welcoming faces.

Again the psalm came back to him: "How shall I sing the Lord's song in a strange land?"

Martin's People

Synopsis: A letter home to my parents in Idaho from the funeral of Dr. Martin Luther King Jr. I was serving a congregation in south Georgia at the time.

Liturgical Calendar: Dr. Martin Luther King Jr. died during the final days of Lent

Scriptures: Isaiah 40:1-31; Psalm 147; 1 Corinthians 9:16-23; Mark 1:29-39

Comment: A true story. This offering is most difficult to categorize. International television and radio broadcasted the event around the world. Even so, it was a most personal time for those in the church and in the street.

Atlanta, Georgia
April 1968

Dear Mom and Dad,

Martin was buried today. It does seem a little strange to call such a famous person by his first name. However, he has had a personal impact on every life in the world. I cannot bring myself to call him Dr. King. He is much too personal.

In a few years, we will see that this has been a very important event. Not happy; just important. Therefore, those of us who were there must put some of this event on paper. The next generations will need to sense what we felt today. We will all need to see some order in the events of the day. Also, I hoped you might be interested.

It was a strange crowd. It wasn't really a funeral, for the mourning was all done Sunday. Well, maybe not all done. For most of the crowd, little emotion stirred. The sadness just blocked itself up inside folks.

It was something of a carnival atmosphere, but with no gaiety. I heard some jokes from a few clowns. Generally, it was just a quiet, comfortable crowd. Most of the crowd on the street was really too young to know how to grieve. The people felt no urgency to grieve and move on with life.

The crowd was huge. I calculated, loosely, about 40,000 to 60,000 standing around in front of the church. Later, I think nearly 120,000 were at the school. The total crowd was around 150,000-160,000. This included all those who just stood along the line of march. The police have not released their figures yet, but this was probably pretty close.

During the procession to the college, I stood in one spot for an hour while the line marched past. Fifteen to twenty abreast, the lines six to eight feet apart. The mourners went by at a good fast walk.

A strange feeling moved in my soul as this unique parade went along. I probably just felt awe at the numbers. The people who came and marched were amazing. Romney, Wilt Chamberlain, Floyd Patterson, Nelson Rockefeller, Bobby Kennedy, Harry Belafonte, Sammy Davis Jr. — all these and more.

After the service, I spent about two hours shuttling mourners back and forth across town. On one trip I had men from California, Seattle, Louisville, Maine, Chicago, Newark, and Kansas City in my Volkswagen bus. Another trip was all airline employees. These were pilots and flight attendants, mostly. These workers had flown in this morning and were leaving this evening. Their airlines had helped them arrange to be in Atlanta for those few hours.

Shuttling people around was fun. I simply drove to where a group of people was walking along. I stopped, opened my window, and waited. Within a few seconds, someone would ask for a ride. I said, "Sure," and they rode. Then several more. Some asked about me. Some asked about Atlanta. Some were curious about Lester Maddox. It was a day of gentility in every sense of the word.

One man stood for more than an hour with a bead of sweat on the end of his nose.

The press was just lousy. The European press and camera crews were the worst. Many of them stood on a flatbed semi-truck trailer in front of the church. They literally stomped on the hands of people who rested against the trailer. They yelled, cursed, and shoved.

A mob of reporters and photographers delayed the cortege as it tried to come through to the church. Some blocked the path of the family and close friends for "just one more."

Imagine the wild newspaper headlines had I done what I felt moved to do. "White man sparks anti-press riot at King's funeral." Deliver me, Lord, from the temptations of the moment.

Really, the mood of the crowd was strange. It was such that neither I — nor probably anyone else — could have started a riot with a fire hose. The press was the only sour note of the day.

An Atlanta patrolman marched past, head high, spit and polished all the way. He had a ten-foot spider web trailing from the spike of his dress helmet.

Atlanta has done a tremendous job in the last three days. The city has been thoroughly impressive by the way it has handled things. The mayor, the police, the churches, and both the black and white communities have come through. Even the weather has been great.

The city government has been very careful to do things just right. It has tried to welcome people without a show of force, but in good style. It helps to have a fine police force. It must be one of the best in the world. They appear to be in the best of form. The Atlanta police showed their training and discipline. Many of them have came to the force right out of the ghettoes.

Governor Lester Maddox boycotted the whole day's affairs. Well, almost. He surrounded the state capitol building with state troopers. They came armed with .50 caliber machine guns. It gave new meaning to the term "overkill."

All kinds of people were here today. The rich, the poor, the proud, and the meek all came. A proud overweight woman in a bright orange dress kicked off her expensive high heels. Then she stood smack on top of a 1968 Lincoln to get a better view.

A meek little lady sat on the front porch of her rooming house and tried to knit. As I watched from a hidden corner, she made error after error. Then she had to pull it apart and redo it each time.

Finally, she just quit and took her knitting inside. When she reappeared, she just sat and rocked and didn't watch.

Fashionable young women stood and talked with their flabby, misshapen mothers. They did not seem to worry about who might see them.

Sharply dressed youths and young men in work clothes stood in groups and eyed the girls for a time. Then they lost interest and just stood. Many uniforms stood out in the crowd. Security, limo drivers, airline and bus employees, waiters and waitresses.

One young man came by, his hair dyed green and wearing a suit to match. Another was in purple, but they were alone. No one seemed to want them.

One color stood out — black. Occasionally, signs of another color could be seen. A sea of black, broken only here and there by the bright colors. The young girl who chose to wear her Easter dress early. Green and purple hair. Hippies' beads and trinkets. Perhaps most beautiful of all, black nuns' faces outlined in white.

At the time the service began, the crowd was so dense it was perhaps a little dangerous. The danger was not from hate. The peril came because we packed so closely together. I moved from one side of the street to the other, and it took 45 minutes.

A young mother stood in the crowd in front of the church. She held a baby and fussed with her small daughter. The older girl was probably about three years old. I stood behind the girl for a while, trying to protect her from the press of the crowd. Finally I asked the mother if I could put the girl on my shoulders.

She glanced at me briefly and approved. The girl and I stood there and talked for about thirty minutes. Finally, the crowd opened a little. The mother said she wanted to take the girl away to a less packed area. I lifted the girl down. The mother said, "Thanks!"

Then she looked at me straight on and seemed to freeze for a moment. "But you're white!" Then she smiled and walked away.

Yep.

All these people came together here for an event they did not fully comprehend. Or believe. Or want to accept.

A few apparently white people stood around in groups, uncertain. It is hard to tell who is white and who is black sometimes.

A middle-aged photographer wore a too-short black filmy dress and a pair of too-big eyeshades.

Dignitaries tried to look somber and politically prominent simultaneously. It may be an internal contradiction.

Bobby Kennedy has wrinkles on his face. Romney is short. Sammy Davis Jr. is a gentleman. He saw that the people bringing the wagon up to the church were unable to get through the crowd. Davis stood on a truck with a bullhorn. Very gently, but forcefully, he convinced the crowd to make a path for the wagon.

McCarthy handled himself as befitting the occasion — quietly, without fanfare, completely sincere.

Another temptation — watch VIPs!

I heard a few ugly words, but it seemed that no one really wanted destruction tonight.

George Wallace opened his campaign here the night Martin died.

Standing outside and across the street, we could hear the singing of the choirs and the congregation inside. It might have been Mahalia Jackson's voice that was so beautiful. I do not know yet. At 100 yards away from the church at that point I could not hear the voice clearly.

The service in the church finished at last. The casket with Martin's body came out and rode on an old farm wagon. It still had the steel-rim wooden-spoke wheels.

Some 20,000 to 30,000 marchers went on ahead when the organizers realized the enormity of the occasion. Then the long trip began.

Away from the Ebenezer Baptist Church. Past the Wink Cleaners. The Lampkin Brothers Cleaners. Haugabrooks' Funeral Home. The Wheat Street Baptist Church, where a huge sign advertises an Easter concert, with a "Cast of 1,000."

Past the Lunch Room. American Legion Post 574. The black-draped Southern Christian Leadership Conference Headquarters, with a small sign out front, "S.C.L.C. Martin Luther King, Jr., President; Ralph Abernathy, Vice President; Andrew J. Young, Executive Director." Through downtown Atlanta. Out to Morehouse College.

What did we do today? Did we honor the man? Or the symbol? No, we need not choose, for we honored both the man and the symbol. The man who became a symbol, and the symbol who was a man.

The slave's grandson was killed while fighting for garbage collectors. He made his last journey on a mule-drawn farm wagon. He rode in a wood box. Martin is gone now. The VIPs have left. The world is left alone with its problem again. Can we solve it?

I don't know about solving all the problems, but I know we made important history today.

Of Bread And Wine

Synopsis: A prayer of institution. Our relationship with Christ is a matter of personal beauty. As clergy, our primary mission is to explore that beauty and expose it to the world.

Liturgical Calendar: Any Eucharist

Scriptures: Isaiah 12:1-6; Psalm 74; 1 Corinthians 1:4-9; Mark 14:1-26

Comment: One necessary of worship, particularly Sunday morning worship, is the need for active mind work. Sunday morning worship ought to be the most exciting time in a Christian's life. This does not refer necessarily to physical activity. It refers to emotional and mental activity.

Gracious Lord, it is right,
    O! Such a joyful thing,
    to give thanks to you,
        (Creator almighty,
            Lord of heaven and earth.)

So now with your people everywhere we give thanks and praise to
    you,
        (Creator almighty,
            Lord of heaven and earth.)

Loving God, we praise you, for you have let us know your created
    world.
    You have also let us know your vision for this world.
        (Creator almighty,
            Lord of heaven and earth.)

Peaceful advocate, you have cried with us
     when we lock ourselves in war with one another.
   Then you have brought us together in peace.
     (Creator almighty,
        Lord of heaven and earth.)

Strong redeemer, you have struggled alongside us
     when volcanos and tsunamis destroy life.
   Then you have brought us together to work to rebuild our
   communities, our lives, our nations.
     (Creator almighty,
        Lord of heaven and earth.)

Heavenly father, you have shared with us our frustrations over the
   rebellion,
     even the deaths of our children.
   Then you have also given us the wonder of the touch of a tiny
   hand and a warm heart.
     (Creator almighty,
        Lord of heaven and earth.)

Sturdy deliverer, you have let us feel the guilt of our sin.
   Yet you have also given us our redemption.
     (Creator almighty,
        Lord of heaven and earth.)

Most of all, speedy redeemer, you have come to us as Jesus, the
   Christ,
     to take on yourself our greatest sin,
        having so much false pride in ourselves
           that we willingly take the lives of others.
   You have born this burden,
     this guilt of humankind, Lord,
        out of your own loving grace.
        (You are the Lord of life.)

Then, precious Lord, you have risen from the tomb,
    and in the act have made the resurrection from sin and
        death a reality.
        (You are the Lord of life.)

We remember the night you gave yourself up for us.
    You took bread and broke it, and gave it to the disciples.
    You said, "Take, eat, this is my body which I have given for
        you. Do this in remembrance of me."
        (You are the Lord of the bread.)

When the supper was over, you took the cup in your loving hands.
    You gave thanks.
    You gave it to the disciples who were gathered close around.
    You said "Drink from this, all of you.
        This is my blood of the new covenant,
            poured out for you,
            for new life in the world to come.
        Do this as often as you choose.
        Drink it in remembrance of me."
        (You are the Lord of the wine.)

So we offer ourselves here as a living sacrifice as we proclaim
    the mystery of faith.
    Christ died;
    Christ rose;
    Christ will come again.
        (You are the Lord of new life.)

Pour out your Spirit on us, loving Lord.
    Make us one with you.
    Make us one with each other.
    Make us one in a ministry to all the world
        until we feast at your heavenly banquet together.
        (You are the Lord of new life.)

We pray through the name,
    and the body
    and the blood
        of Jesus, the Christ.
            (You are the Lord of salvation.)
            Amen.

The Flag On My House

Synopsis: Why I fly my flag.

Liturgical Calendar: Proper 8, Ordinary Time 13, Cycle A

Scriptures: Isaiah 5:1-10; Psalm 111; Romans 12:1-8; Matthew 10:34-40

Comment: The stars and stripes, as a symbol of the United States of America, is intensely personal. It has also been a focus for conflict and debate since Americans flew the first flags. We can recall why we fly the flag.

The flag on my house flies almost every day.
>When I arise, my first act places Old Glory
>>Where God and everyone sees it.
>The breeze spreads and waves the stars and stripes.
>>The gentle wind speaks of life and God and humanity and nation
>>To the early birds and joggers and garbage collectors.
>The flag on my house is a sign of my life,
>>The goodness of all that I know.

>But something more:

The flag on my house is my protest
>Against what I know to be wrong.

The flag on my house remembers the past.
>The red, white, and blue
>>Calls up memories of all the peoples
>>>Who came from other lands to be America.
>My old eyes see in that flag the early peoples who came
>>From Siberia and Fiji,

Guatemala and Norway,
From Spain and China
Morocco and Gaza.

The flag on my house is my protest against
Those who would build a culture
Of degradation and bias
In America.

The flag on my house remembers my family.
The stripes waving in the breeze bring to mind
The generations of youth who came as slaves
From the famines of Wales
Through murderous concentration camps of
Ireland.
The generations of men and women and children
Captured as if wild animals from the forests of
Africa
Bound together by heavy chains
On trading ships across the Atlantic.

The flag on my house is my protest
Against those who would build a wall
To block the poorest of the poor,
Those who come in the name of hope
And redemption.

The flag on my house lifts up those
Who have given their all
For peace and security.
The stars twinkling in the early dawn and the gathering dusk
Tell me the stories of friends and neighbors
Listed on the memorials across the Capitol Mall.
The stars make me pause each day to consider
My firefighter son who served on the *Forrestal*;
My daughter who served the Navy at Sigonella;

My grandson, now a Marine;
My son-in-law, a Navy man.

The flag on my house is my protest
    Against those in high places
        Who pull our nation into war
            Out of a personal hatred of a people;
        Who place our men and women in untenable positions
            Out of an egoist drive for pride and glory.

The flag on my house is a sign of friends and neighbors.
    Holding steady to the staff,
        It tells of believers
            Building the world requires building commerce,
                Operating in cooperation and fairness.

Standing steadfast against the storms and seas and quakes,
    It puts heart and soul into the systems that build lives,
        Ethically,
        Morally,
        Spiritually,
        Righteously.

The flag on my house is my protest
    Against those who steal from the world
        In the name of corporate greed;
            Who pick the pockets of the poor for their own
                Mansions.

I choose to fly the flag of the United States of America.
    The flag on my house is not a sign of support for a government
        That sends my children to die
            To make it possible for big oil to raise their prices
            So that I cannot afford to drive
                To where medical care would be found
                If I could afford medical care.

The flag on my house says life can be better.
  Even in America, life can and should be better.

I do not need to burn the flag.
  Waving the flag is my protest against those
    Who would say I have no right to burn it
      If I choose.

One Fine Christmas Day

Synopsis: Two lovers find each other after a 55-year separation. It is never too late for love.

Liturgical Calendar: Epiphany 5, Cycle A

Scriptures: Isaiah 58:1-12; Psalm 112:1-10; 1 Corinthians 2:1-16; Matthew 5:13-20

Comment: A true story. This pleasant couple was a very welcome part of our congregation. They could easily explain the meaning of love to anyone who would hear them.

Christmas coming up was not an easy thought for Aaron. Christmas should be a time of new birth, of starting over, of new hope. Still, Aaron felt strung out.

Through the Depression, Aaron fed cattle on Montana ranches through the winters of his youth. He did not go to school past the fifth grade, though he did learn to read and write some. He never learned the ideas of youth that we sometimes pick up in school with our algebra and grammar. Aaron did learn about love.

Often nearly frostbitten when the day was done, Aaron found a rancher's daughter to warm him in the evenings. A little handholding and snuggling, with perhaps a dance on Saturday night, seemed to make Marie — and Aaron — very happy.

Aaron knew he had to go someplace else to make some money, so he left town. When he left Montana, Marie soon married another. Aaron was picked off by a girl from Laramie.

Aaron's first wife was a very good person. She mothered three children to adulthood before she died of cancer.

Aaron married another, a long-time friend. She was not satisfied with Aaron's simple lifestyle. He could not earn enough money, so she left him for another after a few years.

Then Aaron married again, a match set up by his oldest daughter. Aaron was happy now, and they had nine good years. A drunken driver shattered his life again by killing his wife in a car wreck.

After another few months of his soul's depression, loneliness and thoughts of suicide began to move in. Aaron tried to avoid the thoughts of Christmas coming. He did not want to buy gifts for his grandchildren. He grew angry whenever he heard Christmas carols on the radio.

Before Christmas, the little weekly paper came out with its headline of "Joy To The World." Aaron became so angry he threw a kitchen chair against the wall. He stomped out of the little house and walked up and down the driveway in pain. He walked until he began to bring his mind together.

What was there to do? What was left? It's either suicide or what? Aaron just felt alone. He did not wish to be alone, to live alone, or to die alone.

Out of this loneliness, Aaron picked up the phone and called a cousin back in Montana. She could feel the loneliness and bitterness in his voice.

"Aaron, you need someone to cheer you up. Why don't you call Marie? She's living in Los Angeles. Her husband died last year. I have her address and phone number."

Battered by life, bruised by circumstance, and bludgeoned by his own errors, Aaron hurt. He could not risk even picking up the phone to make a call.

Instead, next morning he started for Los Angeles in his 1947 International pickup.

Christmas morning, Aaron knocked on the door. When Marie answered, Aaron stood there for a moment, remembering. Then he simply said, "Marie, will you marry me?"

She did, New Years Day, in Las Vegas, on the way to a new life with an old love. Then, and only then, they sent a telegram to her children. They told the sons and daughters to stop by the apartment. They could pick up anything they wanted and junk the rest.

It's never too late to love.

Pete

Synopsis: An altar boy turned Army veteran struggles to make sense of Vietnam, a disheartening return, and a new life.

Liturgical Calendar: Proper 11, Ordinary Time 16, Cycle B

Scriptures: 1 Samuel 1; Ecclesiastes 9:13-18; Ephesians 2:11-22; Matthew 10:34-39

Comment: A true story. This story concerns the inner turmoil of being human in a world struggling with inhumanity. My friend, David Olsen, told me this story. He said it was true and that I could use it in any way I wanted. David died a few decades ago.

David and I enjoyed our little chats. About twice each week, we sat together and I listened to his stories and he listened to my ideas about storytelling. Finally, after several weeks of this, David calmly and carefully lit his pipe. I could tell he was ready to give me something he knew was important. Then he began.

Several years ago, a young man — I knew him only as Pete — came to town. He was a kind of loner. He didn't say much, except at church. He obviously knew a bit about the Bible because he often quoted it. "Jesus said that _____," or "Paul was wrong when he said _____." I knew he must have grown up in the church or something. I thought he was crazy, anyway. I guess the whole town did.

One day it turned out that he had a woman living with him. I guess they never married. She just turned up living with him. He found a few odd jobs in town to support her. He painted a few houses and dug a couple ditches. They stayed to themselves, so we didn't notice what went on between them.

On a Tuesday afternoon some of us were drinking beer over at the tavern. One guy said Pete had been beating her and she had thrown him out. It didn't surprise us, really, because we all knew he was crazy. So we had a good laugh and went home to our own little corners of supposed sanity.

Pete called me a couple of hours later and wanted to talk. We met at the other restaurant while it was closed. He worked there cleaning up sometimes. He had his own key. Pete told me he was leaving town, going back to California. I did not know he was from California, but I could have guessed. He wanted me to hear his story before he left town. I knew he was crazy. I supposed I did not have anything to lose by listening.

Pete had grown up in the hills of northern California. He was the only son of a devout Roman Catholic couple. By his own choice, he served as an altar boy. Later he was confirmed in the church at the proper age. Then he immediately dropped out. Pete looked around at some other religions during his teen years, but they never really attracted him.

The Army drafted Pete during the height of the Vietnam War. As were most of the draftees, he was soon in combat. Pete carried a small machine gun. His group was in the thick of the fighting in the jungle. The Vietcong killed or wounded several while on patrol. Their ambushes slightly wounded Pete a couple times.

After about three months of combat, a very effective force of North Vietnam regulars ambushed Pete's platoon. Pete and the platoon fought back in the way they knew. Soon, though, Pete's ammunition for the machine gun was gone. He threw the machine gun in a ditch. It was useless to him. He grabbed the rifle of a buddy who had already died. Pete and a few others fought their way through the ambush.

Only three of about twenty in the group made it to safety. All the rest died. When Pete returned to headquarters, the commanding officer told him he was responsible for the weapon. Pete would have to pay for it because he was responsible for it and it had not malfunctioned. He didn't have the money to pay for it.

Finally, Pete's turn for discharge came. The Army sent him to San Francisco for discharge. They would give him a bus ticket back to his hometown along with his "mustering out" pay. When he got there, the Army refused. The military would not give him his ticket or his pay. He had to sign a contract to pay for the machine gun he threw away on patrol. Confused and desperate, he finally signed a note. Then, and only then, the Army gave him a handful of cash. He still did not have a bus ticket home. He just had his pay and cash to buy his own ticket.

Pete was not a prudent young man. With a chunk of money and time on his hands, he decided to "do" San Francisco. He promptly got himself drunk. Pete lost all his money, including his ticket money, to a street thief. Really desperate now, he went back to the Army to get some help. They refused. After all, he had separated himself from the Army, so they did not owe him anything. In fact, he still owed the Army for that machine gun.

Pete did not know how to ask for any other help. This veteran of a most foreign war hit the streets of San Francisco again. Nearly starving, he finally met an Orthodox priest who helped him. This man of God made his ministry among the young men and women who walked the streets of the city. The priest fed and sheltered his foundlings. The priest took Pete in.

Then, as the chief part of his ministry, the priest exorcized the demons from the souls of his foundlings. Some of his methods of exorcism were very cruel. Pete had seen cruelty and death in Vietnam, but nothing like this. Some victims were starved or fed rat poison. Others were told they must drink huge amounts of water. Forced sex was common in the group. Some were convinced to cut their own skin to achieve salvation. This was more bitter than anything Pete had seen in Vietnam.

Then, with mysterious and violent rituals, chants, and prayers, the priest and his helper promised salvation. He guaranteed a new life on this earth, separated from all this evil.

With his background in the church, Pete soon began to work with the priest. He helped in the exorcism rites and also the feeding and the sheltering. He was an expert in delivering pain. This had to be a part of the exorcism ritual among the street people.

After a time, he began to have some differences with the priest. Finally, he left San Francisco to seek a new life elsewhere. Pete finally found his way to our little town. Here, he began to make himself a home and he began to pay off the machine gun.

Still, his life had no real meaning. He worked around town a few days. Finally, he began to notice many young men and women around the area. Many were in the same fix Pete had been in San Francisco — lost, lonely, confused, hungry. He knew what his life's mission had to be. The first person he took in was his friend, Mary, a runaway — scared, hungry — and inhabited by an evil spirit.

A few weeks later, I heard Mary threw Pete out. She got a restraining order and a gun. She told him to leave and not come back. After Pete talked to me, he left town immediately. I have no idea where he went. I heard Mary left later. I know she was around for a while; then we just never saw her again.

My friend, David, stopped for a moment to light his pipe, taking just a little too much time before continuing. I waited for the wrap-up.

Pete didn't need to say anymore. I knew who he was and what he was. I knew who I was to him, who he was to me, and to Mary.

David slowly finished his story. He paused a moment, then added, "I guess that's all we need to know about anyone."

A Polish Christmas Carol

Synopsis: A Polish dockyard worker severely injures a soldier on patrol during a time of Christmas violence.

Liturgical Calendar: Christmas 1, Cycle C

Scriptures: 1 Samuel 2:18-20, 26; Psalm 148; Colossians 3:12-17; Luke 2:41-52

Comment: This story might help the congregation understand national revolutions and insurgencies in our world today.

Snow crunched under Private Johann Szesznik's jackboots like popcorn over an open fire. The staccato sound invaded the quiet Gdansk street before Johann appeared. No other sign of life was evident. The Solidarity members and sympathizers hid from the Army patrols that roamed the dark dirty streets. The soldiers simply had orders to go through the streets looking for men and women who might be hiding. They were to bring the civilians to the detention center. There they let the civilian labor bosses put the strikers to work. Johann knew he might also go to prison, or even face execution. He could not dwell on that.

Johann Szesznik was a good soldier for all his twenty years. Good soldiers obey orders. His orders were to bring in the strikers. Johann would rather have been home, or even in the barracks, these last three days before Christmas. Almost anything would be better than walking the streets of Gdansk alone tonight.

Johann stayed on the street. If Johann didn't do his work, he would automatically be found guilty. If Johann did not round up any strikers he found, or if he sided with them, he would only be a deserter. Two who had already deserted this way had tried to flee. When they could not escape, their captain simply shot them. Johann didn't think about that. He was a soldier, and a good one.

Private Szesznik moved from store to store, house to house, peering into the darkened windows. Occasionally, a candle flickered in a small room, showing an old couple huddled together for warmth. Sometimes, he saw a doctor or a priest bending over a sick person. Always, Johann had the sense that someone was watching him. He felt a pair of eyes following his movement along the street. Johann was not afraid of the people he might meet on the street. He knew how to handle them, how to swing his rifle as a club.

The beauty of the city bothered Johann. For centuries, the ironworks and shipyard welders had created a dense smog over Gdansk. This poison held the city like some kind of desperate fist. Now, with the workers striking and the mills and shipyards closed, no smog filtered the light of the street lamps. The moonlight reflected on the snow and created the sense of daylight. If only the town knew peace, lovers who enjoyed the crisp air would fill the street. Older couples would sit quietly at their windows, watching shadows in moonlight. They might even feel the old passions again.

A quiet scratch at the door of a basement apartment hall called Johann to investigate. A small boy stood at the door with his nose pressed against the glass. Occasionally, a small fist melted frozen breath away from his view of the world. Johann waved to the boy from the walk above the door. When the boy waved back, Johann went to the door, opened it, and talked quietly with the boy.

"Hi. My name is Johann. What's your name?"

"My name Milosz. You soldier?"

"Yes, I am a soldier. Do you like the snow?"

"I like to play in snow. I put snow in Daddy's face."

"Is your daddy home?"

Milosz started to answer, then turned and ran back through the hall. Curious, Johann followed. Milosz ran into an apartment near the far end of the hallway.

Johann never saw the man who hit him. He only felt the shock of the club that hit the back of his head. He remembered nothing more.

Daniel Szydlowski dragged the unconscious soldier into his own apartment. Mary Szydlowski stifled a scream as her husband laid the still form on the bed.

"Mary, quick! Go look for blood in the hall!"

Mary wiped up the few drops of telltale red from the hallway floor. Her eyes watched the door where the small nose-circle was fast frosting over. Her vision was of more soldiers coming to their home to take away her husband, the father of her child.

Daniel would go to prison, or to forced labor, or worse, to the gallows. He was a striker, a member of Solidarity, and now he had beaten a soldier. The soldiers would come, and Daniel would be gone forever. The desperate family had only one hope — they would let the soldier die. Then they would bury him someplace where the Army would not find him.

Daniel wasted no time in thinking. Far more important work must be done; important work that comes from deep within the heart of humanity. Quickly and carefully, Daniel took a pair of scissors from the sewing drawer. He carefully tested them for sharpness. Quickly, he cut the already-short blonde hair back from the wounded area of Johann's head. With water and soap and a clean rag, Mary bathed the wound. Daniel found a clean rag and fashioned a bandage that he wound around the soldier's head.

Now, after doing what they could, Mary and Daniel waited. Daniel tied the soldier's hands to the bedframe with cords so he couldn't run away or surprise them.

The next day, Mary and Daniel took the Army uniform off the soldier. They replaced his shirt and trousers with the flannel and cotton of the shipyard laborers. They were still afraid that someone might see the soldier lying on the bed and report him to the police. They hid his grenades in the loose brick of the wall, and his gun found a place in the ceiling.

Together, Mary and Daniel prayed that the soldier would live and that they would not be murderers. Yet, they feared for their own lives if he did live. They knew they might yet have to kill the young soldier to protect their own lives.

On Christmas Eve, when the rest of the world celebrated the birth of the Christ Child and Poland mourned her freedom, Johann began to change. He began to waken, tossing and turning and straining against the ropes that held him to the bed. Johann also began to have fever. Obviously, infection plagued the wound. The infected wound was a more serious danger to his life than two frightened young Poles. Johann had to have medicine — penicillin or sulfa. Daniel knew of only one source.

Daniel went out into the night streets of Gdansk. He looked for the doctor who had delivered both of them and their baby. If Daniel had to, he would tell the doctor that Milosz was hurt and needed the medicine. As he hurried, he avoided the well-lighted street in front of the cathedral. A crowd was gathering for the Christmas Eve mass and too many people stood around.

Surely, the Army would be watching there. The last thing he needed now was a brush with the Army. Daniel bypassed the cathedral and found the doctor. The medical man gave Daniel the medicine without question. The doctor asked a couple quick questions about Mary and Milosz. He reminded Daniel to bring them by soon for a checkup.

Perhaps the doctor knew in his heart something of what was happening. Perhaps he suspected the situation and just doled out whatever medicines he had to whomever asked for them. He didn't give much, but Daniel hoped it would be enough to save the soldier's life.

Daniel started home again through the darkened streets. Gdansk was not so quiet this night as it had been when he surprised the soldier with the board. Tonight, near the cathedral, a group of youths stoned a squad of soldiers.

The soldiers, young and frightened and frustrated, fired wildly in the general direction of their unseen enemy. One bullet, running wild, bounced off a building. It lodged in the side of Daniel Szydlowski, doubling him over with surprise and pain.

Daniel would not allow himself to fall or to quit. He made his way home. He bled a little and feared the soldiers would spot him. If they saw that he had a bullet wound in his side, the soldiers would go to his home and find....

Daniel made it home. The bullet was barely under the skin. The pain was surprisingly mild. Daniel did not try to hide from the Army these last few steps. He just wanted to get home. When Daniel opened the door to his apartment, the wounded soldier was straining against the bedframe. His face showed a rage of pain and delirium.

Mary held Milosz close, allowing her tears to stain his nightclothes. She had put a gag in Johann's mouth to stop him from crying out. His eyes were now wide with a madman's terror.

In a daze, Mary dug the bullet out of Daniel's side and rinsed the wound with soap and water. She reached for the envelope of sulfa to spread on the wound but Daniel wouldn't give it to her. "Mary, if he dies I have wasted everything tonight. Wrap me up. We shall put the sulfa on his head."

Christmas morning came with a gentle snowfall that obscured the sun and gave the children an excuse to play outside. In the cold basement apartment, Daniel and Mary and Milosz talked about how they would spend the day. They did not dare invite friends or neighbors in. It was their custom to act out the Christmas story, complete with lambs and shepherds and cattle and angels. Daniel would be Joseph, Mary would be Mary, and Milosz would be the baby again this year. They could not risk asking other people to come to their apartment to be the shepherds and lambs.

This year, the only person who would be in the room with them was Johann. He lay on the bed, still tied hand and foot. The soldier's fever was going down, and he would be all right. Joseph still did not talk, although Daniel thought he could. Daniel decided, though, that he had to invite this soldier to be a part of the play. Nothing stopped him from taking part except the gag in his mouth. Daniel sat on the side of the bed carefully. He thought long and hard, searching the face of Johann before he spoke.

"I am Daniel Szydlowski. You are Johann Szesznik. I have your identity papers. I do not know why you came to this building. I do not care whether you came to arrest me or to get out of the cold. Anyway, you came. I wish you had not.

"It was I who hit you on the head. It was I who gave you the cut that became infected. I cannot say it is because of you that I have a bullet wound in my side. It was my choice to go out into the streets for medicine.

"I cannot afford to let you go. I do not know what to do with you, tomorrow. Perhaps we shall all pray that we can find a way.

We cannot let you go, for you would bring the other soldiers and arrest us. We cannot kill you because we cannot be killers. All that is for tomorrow.

"Today is Christmas. Since Mary and I married, we have had a little play in our home on this night. We have acted the parts of Mary and Joseph in the Christmas story. When Milosz was born, we had our own beautiful Jesus-child. Last year it was so great, so beautiful with all the candles.

"We have always invited our friends to come and be actors with us. We have asked them to be the sheep and the shepherds and cattle and angels. We cannot do that today. If we asked them to come, some would want to kill you. Others might go the Soviets and turn us in.

"I have trouble thinking of you as a friend, yet at Christmas we really need others here with us. That is the sort of people we are. You are the only one here so I am inviting you to be a part of Christmas with us. You can be the lamb or the cow or, if you like, the pigeons on the roof of the stable. I will take the gag from your mouth, and you can be part of us if you like."

Daniel didn't say it, but he knew inside that when he removed the gag, Johann might cry out. If that happened, Daniel would have to put the gag back and hope that no one had heard. He gingerly began to unwrap the cloth.

Johann was silent when the gag was gone. Mary and Daniel and Milosz became Mary and Joseph and Jesus. The simple basement apartment became the stable while a candle became the star. Perhaps — just perhaps — one could hear a very quiet "baa" or "moo," or sense the flutter of wings.

In the afternoon, Daniel was feeling better about the whole affair. Perhaps it was the day. Perhaps it was the remnant of the Christmas wine they had been saving since summer. Perhaps it was a way of avoiding the unpleasant thoughts about tomorrow.

No matter, Daniel sat on a chair next to the bed and talked to Johann. He talked about his work in the shipyards in the Gdansk harbor. Daniel talked about his simple task of guiding plates of steel into position so the welders could lock the parts of the ship together. "Even you could do it, Szesznik." He talked about life in

Gdansk. He talked about playing football, about Mary and Milosz, and about the snow.

Christmas night, while Daniel and Mary and Milosz slept the sleep of tired escape, Johann struggled with his bonds. He tried to cut the cords by rubbing them against the bed frame slowly, quietly. Johann worked quietly so as not to awaken the others. Early in the morning one came free. Johann slowly, ever so carefully, released his other wrist and his feet.

Swinging his feet carefully over the side, Johann found his boots still beside the bed. Now he was free. Free to leave and free to arrest Daniel and Mary. Free to do his duty as a soldier.

As Johann was finishing lacing his boots, a furor arose in the hall. Jackboots like Johann's clomped on the floor. Shouts and orders and cursing filled the basement with sickening obscenity. The Army was out again, still looking for strikers. They would take them to the concentration camps, or maybe put them to forced labor in the shipyards. In the confusion of these days a man could be sent to a camp quietly. All records of his fate would be lost forever.

This time it was not a random patrol by one or two men. This time it was with lists of names and addresses of strikers. This time it was in six-man squads of heavily armed troopers. This time they knew their mission and their targets.

One soldier beat furiously on the door of yesterday's stable with the butt of his gun. Inside, only Johann Szesznik moved. Daniel and Mary and Milosz froze in terror. The young soldier, still dressed in Daniel's shipyard clothing, opened the door.

"By order of the People's Republic of Poland, we are looking for Daniel Szydlowski!"

Private Johann Szesznik, dressed in the clothing of the shipyard laborer, drew himself to his full height in the doorway. Looking squarely into the face of the squad leader, he spoke.

"I am Daniel Szydlowski. I am ready."

A Little Pushin' And Shovin'

Synopsis: A version of an ancient Indian myth of the creation. Can we really speak of the intentions of the Creator?

Liturgical Calendar: Trinity Sunday, Cycle A

Scriptures: Genesis 1:1—2:4a; Psalm 8; 2 Corinthians 13:11-13; Matthew 28:16-20

Comment: Ancient creation myths do not intend to explain the beginning of the universe. We have more important questions. Is the known universe an intentional product, an accident, or a by-product of some divine activity? What is the role of creatures in the progression of the universe? What is God's intent as the Creator?

The greatest question posed in this story is, "What are the truths of our own creation story?" This story asks the question by narrating a wildly different divine creative activity.

Some time ago — well, perhaps quite a long while ago — the world was just beginning to get its shape.

The earth had been round and smooth like a baby's tummy. Only occasional whirlwinds and little gusts broke the stillness. These breaths blew up bits of dust and leaves and scattered them about.

Huge forests grew everywhere. Giant firs and pines and oaks and persimmon trees made comforting shade whenever necessary. This shade was good for all the animals and birds and insects. The trees even made protection for small plants that needed shade from the hot sun. On the hottest days and the coldest nights the big trees were gifts of life. They wrapped all the little animals against the cold. They sheltered little plants and bugs and birds in their strong branches. Snug and comfy, these rested at just the right temperature.

In those days, a dense, dark forest covered the earth. One of the strongest and most beautiful animals made its home here. Bear lived very nicely, thank you. Berries and fruit and herbs and grass made up most of his summer meal.

Bear ate only one meal each year. Of course, it started when he woke in the spring and it did not end until he crawled back into his den to sleep. Then he did not eat through the long, cold winter. By the time he slept, though, he had gorged himself. He was so fat he could only waddle. He did not have to eat again until next spring.

Bear ate nearly everything close to him. He really didn't want to wander far for his food. That would take too much of the energy he would need to stay alive through the winter. He just ate and ate and ate. Then he ate some more.

He had to roll his folds of fat along to get into his den. In he went, and soon he was fast asleep — sleeping, snoring, and dreaming of next year's big meal.

Bear was very thankful for the forests. Without the forests, Bear would not find food. He would starve to death. But for now, food was everywhere and easy to find. Berries were on the bushes. Fruit was in the trees. Bear had no trouble climbing the trees. His sharp claws helped him run up a tall apple tree to get the luscious fruit. Sometimes Bear even found some insects in a rotted log for dessert — mmm mmm good!

One fall, after Bear crawled into his bed for his really long winter's nap, trouble brewed outside. Sounds of loud snoring came from the den. This signaled peace inside. Peace did not last outside.

Some animals have a tougher time making it through the winter than does Bear. For instance, Coyote.

Coyote didn't sleep that much at once, you see. Coyote did not have that big roll of fat around his middle to keep him going. He got hungry every day and then he needed to eat.

Coyote could not seem to find enough food all at once to eat until he was that fat. After all, who in their right mind would want to sleep that long anyway?

So much excitement in the world kept Coyote from sleeping. To spend the whole winter asleep would be a waste. If Coyote were to sleep that way, he would miss chasing the snowshoe rabbit in the snow. He would not have the chance to tumble down the hill in the snow. He could not roll up as if he were a big snowball. No, sleeping through the winter was not the thing Coyote wanted to do.

A small problem presented itself. If Coyote woke, he would have to find food for himself. For Coyote, food had to come on a regular schedule. He did not mind a little pain, but hunger was not a pain he wanted to learn to tolerate. How was Coyote to find food?

Coyote's biggest problem in finding food was the forest itself. Coyote did not eat the same sorts of food Bear ate. (When Bear was awake, that is.) Coyote did not crave berries and apples and cherries or insects from a hollow log.

Coyote had something a little different in mind. Something with a little meat on its bones. Something like a rabbit would taste about right. Perhaps even a few mice would be nice. Or a quail or sage hen. Now that would be nice!

Lots of these small birds and animals hung around. Coyote ought to find lots to eat in the forest this winter.

That's just where the problem was — the forest. Have you ever tried to run down a rabbit in a thick forest? Trees and bushes and rocks and branches and leaves filled the forest.

It's tough, it is. Very tough. The last time Coyote tried it, he banged his head on a tree trunk while he was running very fast. Just as he was about to catch his supper, his mouth caught a honey-suckle vine. It flipped him tail first into an old rose bush. That hurt!

There had to be an easier way to dine comfortably through the winter. Coyote didn't mind the chase, but Coyote surely enough did mind the bumping and banging and thumping through the forest. If the forest did not have so many trees...!

Coyote's mind jumped at the thought! That's it. I can just get rid of the trees! With fewer trees, I can catch all the food I want!

With fewer trees, the squirrels cannot find a tree to run up to get away. It is embarrassing to chase a squirrel up a tree. It goes up then just sits there and brags about getting away.

So Coyote started the work of getting rid of trees. He wasn't strong like Bear. Bear could just pull them out of the ground. Not

Coyote. He could not push them over. He could not blow them over, though some have claimed he talked enough to do just that.

Coyote could, however, use the tools he had. Coyote had a couple friends who owed him something. Coyote called Wind to help him.

"Wind! Wind, come and blow down the forest! I need to eat this winter! I beg of you. Blow down the forest!"

Wind came and did as Coyote asked him. At least he tried. He blew and blew. He huffed and puffed. Wind blew so hard some wondered if he were the brother of Thunder. Oh, he blew down a few trees. He shook out some robin's nests. Some trees were too strong. Their roots were too deep. Wind just could not blow them all down.

Then Coyote called Lightning. "Lightning! Lightning, come and burn the forest! I am getting very hungry, and when I try to catch my supper, I bang my head on the trees! Help me before I starve to death!"

So Lightning came and started a fire. Lightning found a dry, pitchy log and zapped it hard. He zapped the log so hard it exploded. It showered the grass and bushes and trees around with pieces of burning bark. Lightning started Coyote's fire!

Coyote found that he might have a small problem with Lightning.

You remember, of course, that old Bear had just curled up for his long winter sleep. He had even posted the "Do Not Disturb" sign on his door. He settled cozily into his best sleeping position when "Tthhuummppp!"

Do you remember Lightning and Thunder? And their brother, Wind? Oh, yes, you do. That is the problem with Lightning. Thunder makes that loud "bang" that comes after Lightning throws itself against the earth.

Old Bear was more than just a little annoyed at the interruption. He ripped open his den and stood up on his hind legs to see what was the problem. The whole world was on fire!

His favorite apple tree was burning. The blueberry bushes were going quickly, and the huckleberries were next. What could have started all this? Lightning!

Only Lightning could have done this! Bear called for Lightning to come and help him put out the fire, but Coyote would not let him come.

"Lightning is a friend of mine, and I needed help getting rid of all those dumb trees. I was afraid I would get hungry."

Bear roared now with anger. "Get hungry? Get hungry? If you burn down all the trees, where will your food come from? Sure, you eat mice and rabbits and birds, but where do you think they get their food? You will starve us all to death if you keep on! Now help me put out this fire!"

Coyote and Bear had a good fight that day. The fight went on for some time. Coyote whacked Bear across the nose with a huge limb from an old oak tree. Bear took Coyote in a headlock that would do well in professional wrestling. He dragged Coyote across the earth. This made a trench for running water that would stop the fire. We call that trench the Grand Canyon.

Coyote suddenly borrowed a bolt of power from Lightning. He lifted it high and hurled it at Bear. The two now stood glaring and yelling at each other across the Grand Canyon. Coyote missed with Lightning, but Thunder made his ears hurt so bad he covered them with his paws.

When Bear covered his ears, Wind came up behind and tickled him so much he nearly fell in the Canyon. Bear made a grab for Coyote standing on the other side. The two of them wrestled, grabbed, pushed, and shoved across the earth. Their sweat came so fast and strong it kept the river flowing even to this day.

Bear and Coyote yelled and cursed so much that old Canyon Echo could not keep up. When Bear yelled, Echo had not finished answering Coyote. Sometimes things went so fast that Echo wondered which of the two really expected an answer next!

But they could not get loose from one another! The neighbors pushed and shoved so much and so hard they spread the earth far apart between them. Bear's huge paws clawed and pushed so that he dug Death Valley and the Great Salt Lake. The dirt he dug forced the Rocky Mountains up in the air.

As time went on, all the pushing and shoving made the two giants very tired. They grew more and more frustrated with each

116

other. Neither would give in to the other. With their paws, they tore the earth open wider at the Grand Canyon. Their shouting and roaring and yelping seemed to die down slowly.

As the ruckus went away, both Bear and Coyote were thankful that they were on the good side of the Canyon. Bear was on the north rim, the side with forests left standing. Coyote's den was on the south rim, with open space where he could run and run and run. It would now be easy to catch food.

Coyote pawed the ground so violently that his rear paws dug out the Gulf of California. He dug so much to get a good stance that all that remained between his feet was Panama!

Now come to think about it, the two of them are still there to this day. They meet every night to fight and paw and push and shove. Coyote and Bear make the Grand Canyon a little wider every day with their pushin' and shovin'. Bear fights for peace and darkness and food. Coyote fights for space and light and food.

Whenever Bear stomps his feet a little, we call it another nuclear test. When Coyote shifts his weight, you will read in the papers about another California earthquake.

Bear and Coyote have been out there now a long time, my friends. On a good, clear night you can see the stars over your head. The other creatures stand around and wait for them to give up their fight. They have been there so long that their bodies and their energies have crystallized. They have become something neither of them could ever have dreamed.

Look again. You can see their bodies arched across the heavens yet, strained and taut.

Look again. See? Oh, you call that the Milky Way? Oh....

A Vision Of Peace

Synopsis: A guided meditation prepared for a young mother struggling with her marital relationship.

Liturgical Calendar: All Saints, Cycle A

Scriptures: Revelation 7:9-17; Psalm 34:1-10, 22; 1 John 3:1-3; Matthew 5:1-12

Comment: A true story. A young woman came into my study asking for help. She needed to reestablish her mind in a quiet zone. Her marriage was failing, but she believed she could handle things if she could just find some peace within herself. She thought she could probably reunite with her husband of ten years. I thought a few moments, then told her this story.

Close your eyes and relax. Take a moment to sense your body. Perhaps you can feel the beat of your heart. You may have a little pain some place in your body. Recognize and accept it as part of you.

Let your mind's eye see the picture my words paint. Your mind and body can be at ease. You are safe here.

Our town is small with only a few people. Many dogs and cats live there. Homes and stores and a school provide shelter and care for everyone. Oh yes, and a church. Trees and flowers and birds are everywhere.

The people who live in our little community seem content. You can see them as they go from place to place. They are doing their work, having fun and loving.

Just next to our town is another town of about the same size. It also has schools and stores and a church and homes. The people there seem content as well.

The people in the two towns never seem to get together. They have a problem. Around our town is a brick, stone, and timber wall.

It is high so no one can jump over it to come in or go out. We spend much time working on that wall. We often go to the wall to help. We add a stick here and a stick there.

We make bricks and dry them in the sun. We are very careful the bricks will be just right for the wall. A stockpile of bricks stands ready if we need them. We will use these if the wall begins to crumble.

We don't ask why we build the wall, we just do it because it is part of our life. If a brick comes down from the wall, we replace it. That's our life.

You are taking a brick from the stockpile. Some areas of loose or broken bricks show around the wall. You need to replace a brick on the wall. As you work, a strange thing happens. A man who looks familiar begins very methodically taking the stones from the wall. He pries them free and throws them in a heap. He is taking the wall apart. He works and works, sweating from the effort. He is breaking down the wall faster than you can replace the bricks and stones.

Finally, you quit replacing the wall. Just watching him work feels good. He works and works.

He's down to just the last few bricks. You reach for one of them and rock it until it comes loose. You lift it from its place. You carry it slowly to the discarded heap and leave it there. Then quickly you reach for another brick, and another and another, tossing them onto the heap. Finally only one brick is left. With a shout you grab the last brick and throw it far away. You let your body release and be calm as you watch the brick fly through the air.

You turn away and the man reaches for your hand. Your hands hold each other and you walk. Together you walk through your town. Your senses now find the smells and sounds and feelings of your neighbors and friends.

The town is changing. For the first time the shadow of the wall does not darken the town.

You walk out in the field and into the other town. His hand warms your whole body. You walk ... and walk ... and walk ... and walk....

119

Thank God For School!

Synopsis: A poem of celebration for this institution of parental hope and relief.

Liturgical Calendar: Late August, any cycle

Scriptures: Proverbs 24:3-9, 13-14; Psalm 43; James 3:1-18; Matthew 6:19-22

Comment: Education is a gift from God. It is the difference between humans and the other creatures of God.

My friends, is summer gonna getcha
    'cause the kids will never letcha
    do the things that God
        created summer for?

When the skeeters fall like snowflakes
    and the roof is needing new shakes
    and you've hardly even
        made it out the door ...

When the parents start to mumble and
    the children kinda grumble and
    the teachers pull their hair out
        by the roots ...

Then we know my friend, it's time
    the antsy children go to climb
    aboard the yellow bus
        that heads them off for school ...
Thank God for school!

Have you ever stopped to think
    the world is in a pretty pink
    when the children are not
        trotting off to school?

Bumping heads and bashing noses,
    they are fighting in the roses
    making little sister cry
        and that's the rule ...

Oh, we all know tears of joy
    as we see our little boy
    all cleaned up
        and marching off to school ...
Thank God for school!

I know that I would never ...
    well, maybe hardly ever ...
    go back home
        and do it all again ...

It's not the classes or the books,
    or the teachers' dirty looks;
    it's just the thought
        of crawling out of bed ...

But if I ever find my kid
    cutting classes like I did,
    we'll have a little talk
        behind the shed!
Thank God for school!

The Starfish

Synopsis: Four brief monologues point to the birth of Christ. A starfish clings to life. A Somali woman fights to keep herself and her son alive. An abused woman is freed. God's Christ is born.

Liturgical Calendar: Advent, any cycle

Scriptures: Isaiah 35:1-10; Luke 1:47-55; James 5:7-10; Matthew 11:2-11

Comment: These are true stories. This work lays out the effect of the coming of the Messiah on the world.

Note: These stories are brief. Four different people might read the stories. Discussions might be held between the sections, as in the group study guide. Each story is four small chapters. The chapter headings are identical in the four stories.

The Starfish
The Setup: *The Starfish*

Water is powerful. Every ninth wave coming into the blowhole was a disaster. The tentacles of the nine-inch starfish gripped the rock tightly. It could only wait for the end.

Waves two, three, five, and six were small. They did not even come close to filling the deep, narrow slit in the rock. The water rose a few feet, then receded just as quickly.

One and four were strong. They ran toward the beach resolutely. They came in as two boxers at the opening bell, filled with mission and purpose. Still, they were only mediocre at best. One and four had only small impact on the rocks and sand. They only served to fill thousands of years of endless time. The pattern seemed never to change.

The outflow of waves two and three and five and six and one and four was strong. It was enough to stem the force of wave nine.

These waves were the great protectors. Without this flow of briny seawater back to the deep, nothing could have survived wave nine.

Wave seven just drifted in. It filled the crevice about half way, and left lazily. It placed a few twigs, bubbles, and piles of foam on the sand. Occasionally, it even left a cream-colored sand dollar on the beach. Even a wave will somehow leave evidence of its role in the universe. Then seven was gone forever.

Wave eight was the real culprit. The water of wave eight came in slowly. When it settled in the chasm it hardly covered the sand along the bottom. There it just wasted away. Wave eight seemed to filter out down through the sand. No massive wave or press of retreating ocean rose above the sand. No outflow at all slowed the rush of number nine. Tiny rivulets traced wandering paths through the moving sand. The tiny streams then disappeared before they reach the safety of the ocean.

Number nine came in with all the fury of Genesis chaos. It slammed itself into the blowhole with a muffled roar akin to distant thunder. Then it turned into a distant cousin of a major volcano. It seemed to tear at every bit of order in the universe.

The huge wave exploded against the eroded head of the crevice. The collision threw the water straight up. A water stream spouted skyward through a blowhole. The force of the sea slowly formed this strange nozzle. Thousands of years of pounding surf have had their impact. Millions of years of shifting continental slope have shaped this spectacular spout.

Nine waves. Time after time. Force after force. About every two minutes, a huge wave tore into the chasm. The watery crest tried to wipe the debris from the cut in the rock. The roiling waters scoured off bits of moss, seaweed, and mussels.

The Dilemma: *The Starfish*

The fragile and gentle starfish hung precariously on the lip of the blowhole. Water and the brute force of the ninth wave gave the whole system new life with each immersion.

After every ninth wave, the starfish slowly began to relax its grip on the wet rock. With painful determination, the starfish moved the hairlike fingers on one of its tentacles. This was just enough to break the tension that held it to the rock. Eventually, the tentacle was free to move to another location, downward toward freedom.

Through seven waves the starfish prepared itself to move an arm downward toward the sea and safety. Wave eight played its little hiding and teasing game in the crevice. It came in, spreading into its little hiding places, then left quietly. After wave seven, the starfish recognized some safety and security. It began to release its arms from the dark rock of the ocean beach. The window of opportunity for escape was already gone.

Fourteen seconds later wave nine tore against the fragile starfish arms. The wave crashed against the head of the crevice with a chaotic violence. With the crash, the water threw itself twenty feet in the air. As it passed the starfish, it tore against the strength of the starfish. Those fragile arms strained to hold to the rock, the respite for unknown numbers of starfish over thousands of years.

Frantically, instinctively, the newly loosened arm again gripped the wet rock against the powerful wave action. The opportunity for movement was again lost through panic.

To be free, the starfish had only to relax its grip at the right moment. The fragile creature would be drawn back into its home for renewal. The sea and new life waited. Anything short of complete freedom would be disaster.

Of course, the timing of the release could be wrong. The wave could slam and scrape the starfish against the rough mussel-faced walls of the crevice. The solid rock did not protect the simple, beautiful creature of God's design from its violent personal world. Even free-falling to the sand below would fill the little creature with well-founded terror.

If the separation came at another wrong time, things could go badly. With the ninth wave, the tender starfish might drop down on the sand. Then before it could grab an anchor, the wave could throw it twenty feet skyward through the blowhole.

Bruised and battered on the rocks, the starfish was in deep peril. Slowly the comforting waters washed it toward the deeper sea. It might or might not make it home before the slashing torrent tore it apart. It might meet its own death while drying in the sun.

Salvation: *The Starfish*

The starfish could only hang there, clinging to the rock and to life. To grip survival, if one can, is part of life.

Only God knows how long the beautiful creature struggled against the elements. No one came to rescue this little creature of God from its fate. No salvation came.

Starfish: Two Bodies

The Setup: *Two Bodies*

The boy lay still, barely breathing. His cracking skin found no respite beside the barely functioning body of Miriaj Hassan. The child's ribs barely showed life as they slowly rose and fell. He was so thin, Miriaj could even see the beating of his weak heart within his chest wall.

Miriaj tried only to shield the boy from the hot solar rays pounding the sand. She had little else to offer. Very little food and very little water.

His body was piteously weak from want of food. Miriaj wondered with each breath whether that would be his last. She tried not to think how she might bury him in the desert. The fading young woman had no reserves of strength. She only wanted to get him far enough underground to protect him from birds of prey and jackals.

Arms that should have been throwing rocks, sticks, and balls were limp and wasted. They could have been cuddling puppies. Eyes that should have been teasing brothers or sisters were useless. They were unable to either smile or cry.

Three or four times each day, Miriaj gathered strength to try to feed the small one. Her mind was confused in the heat and by her own hunger. She was not always certain how much time elapsed before she tried another time. She could have tried twenty times each day, but it wouldn't have mattered.

Her own hunger robbed Miriaj of rational thought processes. The fog of hunger created in her a sense of dread. Miriaj had no way to answer any call for support from the child. She did not even know who or what she was. Sometimes she was not certain whether he was her child. She had born a child, about this age. In the heat and sun, her hunger had left her weak in mind and in body. She did not know whether this was her own flesh and blood kin. Maybe. Maybe not.

Her own child might have died. Miriaj might have picked up an orphan along the way. Many children just lay along the road. Some moved. Some did not. She was not certain about this one.

She remembered trying to nurse the young body with the milk of her own tiny breasts. Her body tried, but she finally had to quit. She could not produce any life fluid.

Miriaj constantly tried to make the little body beside her live for another moment. She did not even know if it was a useless effort. Sometimes she thought he might already be dead without her knowing it. Or maybe she was the one who had gone on to a better place. Miriaj had no way to know.

She pulled off a few leaves from the tree which provided them shade. Her mind never questioned whether insects or dirt rested on the slender leaves and stems. That possibility really did not matter. If insects or dirt were on the leaves, she would eat them anyway.

Slowly she prepared the leaves. It was the only potential source of life and protection for Miriaj and the boy. The tree itself was a victim of the waterless waste and of the war. Like the woman and boy, the scrubby tree could do nothing but try to survive.

Miriaj managed to pick up a rock in her weak hands. She pounded the leaves into a pulpy little pile, yellow and barely moist. Then she squeezed a few drops of water from the sand of the seep hole under the tree into the ground leaves. With it, she hoped her paste was real food.

Miriaj groggily attempted to encourage the boy to eat a little of it. He did eat a little. This had been the pattern, two or three times each day, for a long time. She did not know how long.

This starving mother ate the rest of the bitter paste herself. It was bitter, and too dry. She forced the mixture down with pure desperation. She was too weak to know whether she had real choices.

The Dilemma: *Two Bodies*

Miriaj knew she had to make a choice, a very difficult choice. The starving woman was losing the last of her tiny reserve of strength. In another day or two, she would lose her ability to stand at all. The desert would force her to wait in resignation for her own death. She might not even know the moment of the death of the boy. In the desert heat, she might only feel the approach of her own end.

A rumor came that forced her to try to move. At first, she did not believe the rumor. So many passed the rumor along that Miriaj thought it must be true. It gave her new hope for life and survival. Perhaps good people had brought some food to the city.

A city! Even the thought of entering such a strange, evil place frightened Miriaj. Miriaj had been to a city once, as a child. Even then there was fighting along the road. Bloodstains showed along the streets and in the stores.

Miriaj had seen her own mother beaten and raped by violent young men. These violent boys took turns with Miriaj just as they did with her mother. No more than animals, these wild youths. The same fighters and rapists ignored her father dying in the street from their bullets.

The desperate young woman feared this alien place of houses, buildings, schools, and police. She knew nothing of living with such things. What would it be to sleep again at night beneath a roof? Besides, it had to be a least eight or ten days of walking. Miriaj doubted she could make it.

She might find food if she did. Food for herself and the boy. If she could get him to the city before she died, someone might have food for him.

As Miriaj pondered what to do, she slowly ground several days' ration of leaves from the tree above her. She thought she could last several days on the small handful of paste.

This was nearly the last of the leaf paste. If she could reach real food, it would be worth the work. She at least had to try, both for herself and for the boy.

Miriaj could not bring herself to leave this boy beside her. At this point, whether or not he was her son was an unimportant matter. He was a human life. God and the war had committed his entire life to her care.

Salvation: *Two Bodies*

Miriaj Hassan struggled to mix her cold, bitter paste of leaves and dew. She passed out from her exertion in the heat. She did not know she was very close to death. Miriaj could not stand and walk, even with the fresh supply of leaf paste. Death was very close.

The Marines scooped up the nearly lifeless bodies. The fighters laid the limp figures on rough blankets on the hard bed of the camouflaged six-wheel truck. She stirred, ever so slightly, from the touch of rough hands. A pair of wasted bodies on a camouflaged truck in a forlorn desert had almost no impact on life in the world.

In this new community of several bodies on the truck, something good happened. Perhaps the angels might, just might, have smiled a little.

The young Marines were ready to kill or be killed. They were ready to accept death in war. Now they began to mop her face with water. As they poured water on her, they could see her skin smoothing out the cracks.

The Americans gave Miriaj and the little one sips of a white soupy mixture. It was UNICEF life in liquid form. They drove slowly along, stopping occasionally for yet another unknown form. The Marines continued gently urging life-giving fluid into the bodies of Miriaj Hassan and the boy.

The Marines had volunteered for military service, with life or death at any moment. Little could they know their most heroic and important act as soldiers might be this one. They saved two starving human beings from death on the hot deserts of Somalia. On that day, other Marines saved the lives of many people on the great plains of Africa.

"No one has greater love than this, that a person lay down their own life for that of another."

Starfish: The Abused

The Setup: *The Abused*

Every day of Mary Ann's life was another day of hell on earth. She tried to do right. She really tried. Sadly, she came again to know this marriage was a failure, just like the others.

Some of her other relationships were not really marriages. In her mind, living in the same building did not count as a marriage. The hurt was all the same, though. Most of her men did not need a license to abuse her.

Evenings had little variation. Mary Ann waited for her man to come through the door. He would carry a couple of six packs from the convenience store. He usually had one six pack inside and two six packs outside his body.

Her man was always drunk enough to abuse her. She always expected him to beat her into senselessness. After the abuse, her so-called lover fell into a stupor that passed for sleeping.

She was not too worried about being raped. Mary Ann would only be beaten and verbally abused. He had not done anything sexually for months. Alcohol does this to a man. The woman only gets the blame.

Her man slept the deep sleep of a drunken stupor. Mary Ann took her time fishing through his billfold for enough money for rent. Then she found a little for food. Occasionally, a little was left to pay on the medical bills that mounted up with the beatings. The terror was costly.

By now, Mary Ann did not worry about the future. Nothing mattered beyond the next day. Even death itself would have been a welcome respite from her own failed life.

After her children grew up, her first husband died. He was the love of her life. Their twenty years of good marriage did not prepare her for her next long years. Each of her other relationships ended the same, marriages or not. She simply found some other way to go to another location. She always found a different man, another situation, and another hopelessness.

This time it was bad. Awful. The man was a monster. He even occasionally tied her to the bed while he tried to rape her. He always failed. Perhaps it was time to leave him. She could find someone else.

Why should she try again? Each time she had gone from something bad to something worse. So why try? What could possibly be worse than this? This time Mary Ann really did not want to know.

Dilemma: *The Abused*

Mary Ann cried the tearless woe of the hopeless. Her desperation was such that she could only hope for sudden death. She began to wonder how she might die.

Mary Ann was not terribly concerned about her own children. They could survive without her. Her daughters had families. Their homes were good ones with good men.

Her son, though, was a heroin addict. He was twenty years old, homeless, wandering someplace across the country. If he chose this lifestyle, it was what it would be. It was a choice for him and him alone. She was not strong enough to help him find a new life.

Mary Ann's deepest real hurt now was her own shame. Her record showed a complete failure at her own life. She should have done better.

This desperate woman had been the valedictorian of her class. Later she attended business school. She was a regular church attender, faithful in prayer through youth and twenty years of marriage. She must have done something terribly evil in her life. There had to be some horrible deed or thought for which she must now pay. She often struggled with God. What was so bad about her life?

Maybe Mary Ann had not appreciated her good first marriage. It was a good time, a joy and a blessing. Probably God was punishing her for her frustration with her children as they grew up. What parent does not become a little frustrated? Or maybe not.

Mary Ann mostly waited now. She waited for the end that could not come too soon. The grave would come as a release.

Salvation: *The Abused*

Mary Ann could not have known what would happen next. She could not have asked for it. All her years of violence and resignation did not prepare her for such a turnabout. As she waited alone, telephones rang persistently. Long lines heated to bright red along the Pacific coast from Canada to Mexico. Mary Ann's desperate cries had been heard from Seattle to San Diego.

Mary Ann's daughters heard her cries for help. The sons and daughters-in-law of her abusing husband turned their support to their father's wife. Then, in the spirit of Jesus, they pooled their meager savings. The next generation did what they could for her. They chose to save the woman who had given the daughters life.

Putting together all they had, the far-flung family began to work together. The family worked in the name of humanity. Yet, it was Christmas. Many things happen at Christmas that might not happen any other time of year.

Jerry, the oldest son-in-law, flew from Seattle to Los Angeles. He rented a truck with an already burdened credit card. Early the next morning, Jerry and a couple of cousins showed up at Mary Ann's house. Mary Ann could only sit and cry.

They loaded Mary Ann and what was left of her furniture in the truck. That took all day. In the evening, the truck and the new dreams left for Oregon.

Starfish: The Eternal Attempt
The Setup: *The Eternal Attempt*

It seemed like a waste. It really did. The Creator has a loving purpose. Time and again, God tried to make the world the best place possible for those whom God loves. After all, it was a gift for the highest creation, people with heart, soul, mind, and strength.

Time and again, God's people wrenched the divine heart. Their violence toward each other frustrated God. God struggled inside with the seeming unwillingness of people to talk with each other. Somehow God wondered if these people would ever know about love and peace and collaboration.

The ones on earth whom God loved resisted sharing the gifts of life. A God who loved the people had given the gifts.

Sometimes they challenged God's intent. There seemed almost nothing left to do but give up. The only possibility gave the people the terrible things they chose for themselves and others.

Adam and Eve chose separation from God and from each other. Adam and Eve hid their inner beings from each other and from God. They hid their guilt and distrust from the God who created them and loved them. God gave them a home away from the garden of Eden, complete with leaves for clothing. God always found a way to start over.

131

God also found that starting over was not enough. The Creator also had to witness more of the inhumanity of humankind. Noah's neighbors destroyed not only their neighbors but also themselves. Only Noah tried to remain faithful. Only Noah tried to keep his personal relationship with his God and with the other creatures of God. God allowed the rain to wipe out all but Noah and his family. Yet the Hebrews did not get it. The descendants of Noah again turned from faith.

In captivity in Babylon, the Hebrews again turned their backs on their own faith. They went off to worship the false gods of the Tigris and Euphrates River Valleys. In the land known now as Iraq, the Hebrews again turned away. They rejected the Creator who made them, loved them, and redeemed them. God let them live among the Babylonians as slaves for more than 200 years.

The Dilemma: *The Eternal Attempt*

Now, what to do? Rome was at the height of her power. Half the people of the world were directly or indirectly affected by decisions made in Rome. If Rome chose war, war ravaged the world. When Rome chose to build highways, paved roads sprang from and to the far corners of the earth.

God knew Rome could decide to wipe out the little group of Jewish people. They were a tiny nation God chose to display the Creator to the world. If Rome chose to wipe out the Jews, the people God loved would just disappear. If so, it would be very hard on God's own choices. God had started over before. It seems God did not relish starting over repeatedly.

From the garden of Eden, Adam and Eve had started over almost instantly.

The rains fell on Noah and the ark for only forty days and nights.

The Hebrew children wandered in the wilderness of Sinai for only forty years. Then they started over in their new land.

The Babylonian captivity lasted over 200 years. Another attempt to warn and redeem the people might last for 1,000 years. Perhaps it might even be 2,000 years.

Salvation: *The Eternal Attempt*

God had a promise to fulfill. The birth of Jesus took place something like this. A young, faithful woman, Mary, was engaged to an older man, Joseph. They lived in Nazareth, in Galilee.

One night while Mary slept a deep sleep, the angel whispered she would have a son. The angel said she should call him "Jesus." He would save the people from the hurts of their own lives.

They told Joseph, also, that Mary was pregnant. This made Joseph's task very difficult. Joseph knew he was not the child's father. He was a compassionate man, but did he have limits to his compassion?

He could not allow any harm to come to the woman he loved. Perhaps that is why Mary loved him so much. Joseph decided to simply call off the wedding.

Joseph knew he was not the father. It could not be. To call off the wedding quietly was the decent thing to do. Anything else would have meant shame, if not death, for Mary. Joseph could not let that happen to the girl he loved.

Again the angel came to Joseph. The angel convinced him to take Mary to be his wife. He willingly did. It was a beautiful act of love. It was a fitting act for the family of the person who would be God's love in human form.

Then the time came for the birth. It was also time for Joseph and Mary to make the journey to Bethlehem to pay the tax. Joseph and Mary went, but not because they must. They could have paid someone else to take it and report their family status.

To simply send the money with one of their relatives would have been a violation of their heritage. Joseph and Mary could feel no part of the family pride if they only sent someone else in their place. They must travel to the holy city for themselves. They had to see their ancestral home, the city of David. Mary and Joseph did it for David. The young family went for Isaiah and for Moses. The loving couple went for their own future. The loving couple did it for the Messiah.

When they reached Bethlehem, the inn was full. Mary and Joseph found space in the stable. When the infant was born, Mary wrapped the baby in simple cloths, then laid him in the manger. God's love came to earth in human form.

At that sacred moment, it seemed that all the heavens themselves opened up. The world sang to welcome the newborn child, the Prince of Peace. The hope of the world rested in him.

Amen.

The Strangest Dream

Synopsis: A pastor's duty disturbs the rest of a working woman. Could the pastor foresee the result of his actions?

Liturgical Calendar: Lent 3, Cycle C

Scriptures: Isaiah 55:1-9; Psalm 63:1-11; 1 Corinthians 10:1-13; Luke 13:1-9

Comment: A true story. We often fail to see the overall consequences of our well-intentioned actions. Every action has consequences for which we must account.

Pastors around the world know trouble when they hear it. The phone or the doorbell ringing after 11 p.m. invariably brings a resigned, "Uh, oh."

This is always true on a Saturday night. It means that someone is in a world of hurt and I will end up getting dressed and going to them.

The sound of frantic and insistent pounding at the front door brought me finally to my senses. Saturday night, nearly midnight. Sleep was precious, and I was tired.

At the door stood a young woman from the community. I knew her only slightly. Sometimes we spoke when we met on the street. She lived about four blocks away. Rapidly, she poured out her story.

Ramona and her husband had been driving around drinking. As is common, they got into a big fight. Yelling, crying, slapping. She got out of the car when things were at their worst.

He tried to run her down as she ran across the park. Now she was afraid to go to their home alone. She feared he would be there waiting for her. As the only acceptable alternative she knew, she went to the door of the parsonage, our home.

She wanted most of all for me to take her to her home. Then I should see to it that she got into the house safely. After much hesitation and a dozen or so lame excuses, I finally agreed to go with her. I told my wife, Donella, that if I were not back in an hour she should phone the police.

Only a single patrolman held the town together at night. He kept a loose watch over the town. A scratchy radio telephone in his car aided the patrol.

The lady and I finally drove up to her house. Sure enough, her husband was there. However, just as we drove up the patrol car stopped behind us. When we left our cars, the guard from the potato products plant across the street came over. He wanted to see what the excitement was. Then a few neighbors appeared as if by magic. This much activity on a quiet town street at night was highly unusual.

For over an hour, the couple talked on the steps of their house. They argued and cried. The rest of us just waited in the street for some clue that the crisis was past. Finally, I told the officer I needed to call my wife. He said I could use his radio telephone. I think he did not want me to leave. He dialed the number for me and handed me the receiver.

A woman's voice, deep with sleep, came on the line. "Helloophmm?"

"Donella, everything is all right. The city cop is here. It's all right. Go on back to sleep."

"Hoommnnpphhgnk?"

"Honey, it's okay. Just go back to bed."

"Hwasuuingnnhfkl?"

"Honey, everything is all right. Just go back to bed. I will be there pretty soon. The cop is here. Don't worry. Good night." I went back to joking with the cop and watching the excitement on the stoop.

About fifteen minutes later, a parishioner appeared. Donella had called him and asked him to check on me. Because I had just talked to Donella on the radio telephone, I assured him that everything was clear.

We talked for about another hour before the couple finally went inside. The husband had sobered up a little. I went on home.

Donella was not a happy camper. She was mad. She was relieved. She said, "You could have at least called! When Joe didn't call me back I just knew something terrible had happened! I didn't know what to do!"

No amount of sweet talk could help her understand that I did call. She must have been so asleep she did not remember talking to me.

Next morning, at that same potato products plant, one of the inspection line workers seemed a little uncomfortable and confused. Some of her coworkers asked her what was troubling her. Her husband had died a few months before, and they wanted to be as supportive as they could.

"I have decided to quit taking these sedatives the doctor gave me after Charlie died. Last night I took some and I had the strangest dream...."

The Ladder

Synopsis: A youth learns the responsibilities and risks of manhood. The challenge of picking apples.

Liturgical Calendar: Proper 6, Ordinary Time 11, Cycle A

Scriptures: Genesis 18:1-15; Psalm 116:1-2, 12-19; Romans 5:1-8; Matthew 9:35—10:8

Comment: A true story and a true miracle. Lots of discussion fodder here for any age group.

My own children talk a lot about the old days. According to them, we genuine old-timers know nothing of airplanes. Dial telephones and printed material are alien to them. They talk about how easy things were in their olden days. Apparently, that was especially true for their parents.

It seems that raising youngsters back in the middle of the twentieth century was much easier than it is now. It also seems that growing up now is so much more difficult than it was back then. Today's youth believe it is even more violent today than it was in the good old days. I am not certain I can agree with that.

I know things have changed. We shipped a box to our daughter and son-in-law in Arizona. I put it into our little pickup, along with the little hand truck.

When we arrived at the shipping company store, I took the package out of the pickup. The hand truck allowed me to wheel it into the store. I picked it up and placed it on the scale in front of the clerk.

The clerk griped and moaned because the box rocked a little. She spent several minutes hemming and hawing and complaining. It seems we interrupted her little siesta. After she had her gripe about interrupting her nap, she pasted a label on the box. I stood the box in the corner for the driver to pick up later. That should make the clerk happy. I figured wrong.

Now she really started beefing at me. It seems I had violated a company rule: At least two people must handle any carton that weighs more than seventy pounds. Our box weighed about 85 pounds. I could have carried it in under my left arm.

Now think about it. When I was the age of that clerk, things were lighter. A carton had to weigh at least 200 pounds to qualify for additional help. As a growing boy, I loaded thousands of hay bales weighing over 125 pounds on trucks. A few hundred every year weighed over 200 pounds. I loaded them all by myself. Of course, I could not throw the heavier bales more than eight feet high on the truck. That was not a problem. It was the way we lived.

Things have changed. Not always for the better. In the midst of change, some things need to stay the same. Commitments, for instance.

I was about twelve or fourteen when I went to work for Roy Wilkerson. I liked old Roy. He had been an infantryman in both WWI and WWII. He claimed to have fought at Verdun, in North Africa, and in the Battle of the Bulge. German poison gas hit our hero hard near Verdun.

I worked a lot for him. I stacked hay, plowed, and milked cows. I irrigated corn and hay. I picked fruit, mostly apples and prunes. Picking fruit for Roy was an onerous job. It was a job I never did like.

One Saturday, in the fall of about 1954, he asked me to pick the apples. He had a dozen trees growing close to his basement house. I figured I could handle a few boxes of apples. Picking fruit was an onerous job, but I needed the money, so I agreed.

Roy had a half-dozen very tall trees. He apparently never met an apple tree he did not like. Emotionally, he could not bring himself to prune them. He just let them grow. Some of these trees were well over twenty feet tall.

Roy had another problem for me. His home was just about 100 feet or so from the major irrigation canal. The water from this canal irrigated several thousand acres farther down the hill.

Pocket gophers just love to excavate near canals. They try to get close to water with their tunnels whenever they can. If their tunnel happens to run below water level, the water seeps through into their little homes. It spills out, fills their passages, and floods the neighboring land — and the orchard.

When I climbed on Roy's fruit ladder, I never suspected a problem. The tree, a ladder, and a bucket were all the tools I needed. What more could one need to pick apples? Okay, let's do it.

An old wooden fruit ladder is a rickety thing at best. Even a new ladder was tricky and shaky. Roy never had a new ladder.

Roy's ladder was sixteen feet tall. It had wobbly rungs on one side. The two boards running up the ends of the rungs spread about four feet apart at the bottom. The legs came close together at the top. A tripod leg supported the back side of the ladder. The tripod leg was a single hardwood two by two hinged to the rung side at the top.

Typically, home orchard ladders had a third leg which had been broken and repaired a few times. These modifications only made the ladder heavier and stronger. Roy had wired and bolted an additional board next to the third leg to make it sturdier.

I hooked my bucket on my belt. As I climbed the ladder, I picked apples as I climbed. It took several trips up and back down to pick the fruit and empty the bucket.

I finally worked my way to the top of the ladder. Standing with one foot on the next-to-top rung and one foot on the top of the ladder, I was ready. I could almost reach the top of the tree. No matter how I tried, I could not get the last dozen apples. I was not personally long enough.

With just a little stretching I could get one more. This last apple was bright and red, large as a softball. I really had to get it into my bucket.

It seems this was one too many. A little shiver in the ladder panicked my bones. The shaking gave me a vivid understanding of what was about to happen. My thoughts were simple. *This probably will not be good!*

I should have been in an Olympic ice dancer's exhibition. My foot skipped from the top of the ladder to the next rung. Quickly. That might have saved my life, but something was still wrong.

My mind's eye saw what was happening in the Wilkerson orchard. The third leg of the ladder was sinking into a mud hole.

Those lousy pocket gophers were about to have their day at my expense. The ladder was not going fast, just sinking. It went slowly, like a pencil in an algebra test. I just went along for the ride.

The vision of those little gophers enjoying the scene still riles me. I have a lasting image of those little fellows enjoying the view. They are sitting back in their little lawn chairs, sipping lemonade. As I begin to fall over, applause fills the orchard. Then little Olympic judging signs begin to appear in their hands. "6" "8.5" "5.2" Practice will make perfect, I suppose.

Some lessons of history came to mind. Some Old Testament folks have been particular favorites of mine. I think of Noah, for instance. Old Noah didn't have much choice. He really did not want to build that boat. He finally just had to make the commitment. That's when things got tough for him.

Noah tried to get everyone on board, but they refused to come. Noah wanted the relatives to bring the animals with them. They rebelled. I suspect they did much fussing and moaning and groaning. Some folks do not like to share things — lifeboats, for instance — with animals. Then the rain started to flood them out. Suddenly, all the out-of-work relatives wanted to get on board.

The people celebrated Noah's commitment. When it looked as if the ladder was going completely into the mud, Noah stayed on. His commitment to his Lord stayed strong as his ladder began to sink. He rode it down. Talk about needing a longer ladder. Noah knew about the need for long ladders.

And Moses. Moses said, "Sure, Lord. I will be on your side. Just tell me what to do. Piece of cake!"

The Lord told Moses what to do. Before the Egyptians started coming across the desert, many Hebrews were reluctant to come along. However, the Hebrews who had opted out earlier soon wanted to be part of the parade. Then the Hebrews saw the horses, chariots, camels, Humvees, and armored personnel carriers of the Egyptians. I know what Moses was thinking. "Oh, Lord, this ladder is sinking plum down into that gopher hole. I am going down along with it. This isn't quicksand, is it?"

When King Saul needed someone to go put a whuppin' on Goliath, David volunteered. He apparently had not learned the first lesson of military life — never volunteer. I guess he was too young. It was his first experience in the military. Yet, he made his commitment. Sticking with it was important.

Goliath jerked a telephone pole out of the ground so he could beat on little David. I know what David was thinking. "Oh, Lord, this ladder is sinking fast. I don't know if I can hold on. Here, Lord. You hold on for me. At least hold the bucket."

What was Jesus was thinking when he met Herod and Pilate? They had all their armies and guards armed with hammers and spears. I know what I would have been thinking. "Oh, Lord, this ladder is no dad-gummed good. Can I get one with a longer third leg? Don't show up with any nails. I know about them."

It seems that every one of them was promised to someone. Then, when times were tough, they made a choice. They could bail out, or they could ride the ladder down. It's a choice we all have to make — to bail off or ride the ladder down.

As the ladder went on down, I balanced on that next-to-top rung. The third leg and the left leg of the ladder were both sinking into the gopher work. Fine plumbers, those little fellows.

I could hold on to a stout limb of the tree. The ladder was pitching me forward and sideways, slowly. As I neared the ground, the limb broke. I was still standing precariously at the top of the ladder. At about six feet, I lost my balance and just fell. I could jump a little, so I landed feet first, and backward.

My commitment was to Roy and his apple trees. The job had to be done. It was, I supposed, a lot like getting married. Hang on, sweet lips. Or maybe it was like any other commitment. When the ladder starts to sink, that is the time to hang on. David and Noah and the rest did. Jesus did it for me. How could I do less?

I landed on my feet and rolled back onto my head. The somersault was not pretty as I rolled on over. I would not earn an 8.5 on that one. Lying flat on the ground, I gingerly moved each leg and arm just to see if I still could. Then I held my head in place so I could roll over and check out my neck.

The apples from the bucket spilled all over the grass. Oh, well. As I got up I knew only that I had kept my end of the bargain with Roy. That was enough. Life demands that we keep our commitments.

Noah did it. Moses did it. David did it. Jesus did it. He had a little rougher time, but he did it.

So did I.

Ducks, Frogs, And Mud

Synopsis: One of God's little communities nearly dies, then comes back to life. The community itself makes it live.

Liturgical Calendar: Christ The King, Cycle A

Scriptures: Ezekiel 34:11-16, 20-24; Psalm 100; Ephesians 1:15-23; Matthew 25:31-46

Comment: This writing has been fun for a long time. All ages love to participate.

Note: This could be used as a readers' theater with actions. Actors can dress the parts or just wear signs naming their role. Do not be in a hurry. Can be presented with almost no preparation time.

Every creature has within itself a beautiful nature that fits in God's creation. A human being or poplar tree or metamorphic rock or Percheron horse shares this heritage. The Creator equips every-thing for a particular role in things. "Ducks, Frogs, And Mud" ex-plores this relationship.

This presentation is appropriate for presentation to and by any age group. It is also appropriate for any venue, faith group, number of participants, or literacy level. The major variation suggested might be in selection of costumes. It has been a monologue occa-sionally — both as a monologue sermon and a monologue with actions. It has been presented with no character sounds and with active character sounds and/or dialogue.

"Ducks, Frogs, And Mud" has been presented with no rehearsal at all as a readers' theater. Each character read the lines that tell of their actions. It has worked with the actors simply performing their parts for the first time as they act out the parts. It has been pre-sented after hours of practice and days of costume preparation. People of all ages have filled the roles. We have even included pets on occasion.

The major reader might be in position on one side of the stage. A second reader could be on the other side literally telling the actors what to do. This play could literally be purchased and immediately go to performance. Only a few moments of preparation would be required.

Multiple readers are appropriate. Different readers might read the action narratives for the different characters. Many people might easily be involved in the presentation. Sections of a large crowd could be given different roles to play. No real limits should be enforced.

This story will be as meaningful to the reader and performers as it is to the audience. Therefore, the existence of spectators is irrelevant. Every person may be included as a performer. All these scenarios have worked well. Use your creativity. No value is found in holding back your own genius.

Themes

Primary Theme — personal responsibility

Secondary Themes — stewardship, church growth, social action, ecology, group spirit

As with any story, it would be an error to attempt to define the whole meaning of this narrative. Each listener and watcher, including the performers, will find within the story their own meaning. Letting that stand is best. Often, we cannot identify this personal meaning well enough to openly define it.

We must make one important note here. Please do not ask what the author has in mind for the story. Only ask what you, as a witness, find in the words and actions involved. If you accept the power of the Holy Spirit, allow God to lead wherever God chooses.

Characters

Minimum number — one (Reader)

Maximum number — unlimited

With additional people for roles, simply add more names to any of the character species. An additional duck would be all right. It might be David or Dravina Duck. Additional people might be placed in roles as Otters, Skippers, Fish, Crawdads, Turtles, or

Ducks. If children of any age are in the group, we may include them in the other roles, as well. Practice is probably irrelevant. Just have some fun.

Some characters will be more appropriate for people with certain types of disabilities. For instance, a person in a wheelchair could easily play Fonda Fish. Use your imagination. Also, if the gender needs to change for any character, change it.

> Reader — one or more who can read clearly, loudly, and pause at appropriate places for action to take place; no rush at all to complete the story, but timing is important.
>
> Darrell Duck — hard working, leadership type, a good thinker
>
> Toby Turtle — slow and hungry
>
> Oliver Otter — playful, sleek, yuppy(?)
>
> Carol Crawdad — busy, busy, busy; moves slowly, but keeps moving
>
> Sally Skipper — jumpy, skips around, slender
>
> Fonda Fish — the mermaid of the bunch, rather shy

Costumes

> Reader — use anything that works; be creative
>
> Darrell Duck — a duck bill on the face, swim fins for the feet, and a paper cone tail
>
> Toby Turtle — a GI surplus helmet, football helmet, or galvanized tub on the head
>
> Oliver Otter — streamlined clothing (Spandex?) for riding bicycles or swimming
>
> Carol Crawdad — large pair of pliers in each hand
>
> Sally Skipper — extra legs and arms; if on crutches, wrap them in black paper(?)
>
> Fonda Fish — wrap lower torso in a large towel; possibly someone in a wheelchair

Several alternatives to costumes come to mind. The performers might simply wear signs hung around their necks stating their roles in the performance. We might make large crowns stating the various roles. Facial or full body masks could be worn.

146

Props

The pond covers most of the performance area. This can be something visual or perhaps only in the imagination.

The dam should be something solid, wide, and tall. Use anything appropriate, such as a table, a pulpit, a wall, or perhaps just in the imagination. Be brave and create.

The use of color is good.

The stage may be populated or not before beginning the reading. Your choice may depend on the abilities of the performers and the choices of the director. Some or all of the performers may be on stage from the beginning. The performers may wander in slowly over a period, before or after the Reader begins.

(Reader or person acting as narrative assistant may need to point out the pond and dam and other props.)

Reader: Once upon a time, I knew a pond. It was not too far from here, I think. Perhaps a little farther. Perhaps a little closer. This pond was home to a large family.

(Play this scene positively. Smile at each other, obvious support for each other, like massaging shoulders or pats on the back.)

Reader: This family was just about typical, but not quite. Lots of different sorts of creatures lived there, different sorts of dreams and different sorts of problems.

(Darrell Duck slowly works his way to a command presence on the stage. Others turn to face him.)

Reader: This little family was all the animals of the pond. All the animals learned to live with each doing their own little thing. As they lived together, each added something from their own life that made life good for all of them. One of God's creatures at the pond was a sort of leader. He named himself Darrell Duck.

Darrell: *(quacks loudly and struts around)* Quack. Quack.

Reader: Now, Darrell Duck had much duck work to do. His work was something that God had called Darrell Duck and only Darrell Duck to do. He was the one who spoke out a lot and made sense when he spoke. Normally, he worked very hard in the pond. All the other animals liked him and listened to him.

(Darrell Duck looks carefully around the pond.)

Reader: All day long, beginning with the earliest sunlight, Darrell Duck would slip into the water, swim to a likely spot, and tip tailside-up into the water. It was a very funny sight.

(Darrell Duck turns tailside up and moves around with nose on the floor and tail in the air.)

Reader: Then, with his tail in the air, Darrell Duck would use his shovel-like bill to do God's work. He pushed it rapidly along through the nice mud on the bottom of the pond. He used his bill this way every day. He looked for worms and roots and other fine things to eat. He found them in the mud on the bottom of the pond. He fed himself this way. He also helped keep the pond clean and alive. Darrell Duck did not work alone. Darrell Duck also worked with Toby Turtle.

(Toby Turtle moves slowly and looks sleepy.)

Reader: Toby Turtle moved very slowly on land.

(Toby swims around the pond slowly, cleaning it up a little.)

Reader: In water, he was very effective. Toby Turtle swam around nipping plants and moss. He cleaned unwanted growths from the tree roots that grew from the oaks along the banks of the pond. Toby Turtle ate the weeds that grew in the pond. These weeds would have clogged up the water if they grew unchecked.

(Toby Turtle slowly assumes sunbathing position.)

Reader: Sometimes, Toby Turtle would just lay out in the sun and relax. If the water was a little cool, the nice, warm sun shining on his shell made him feel so good. Perhaps Oliver Otter had the best time of it.

(Oliver Otter is self-satisfied. He uses water as a mirror to admire himself.)

Reader: At least he thought so. Oliver Otter spent most of his time just playing, he thought. His play was very good for the life of the pond and for God's other creatures.

(Oliver Otter dives and swims. He does it repeatedly.)

Reader: Oliver climbed to the top of the bank and paused to be certain everyone was watching. Then, with much chattering and tail wagging and squealing, Oliver slid down the bank into the water. Then he swam to get to the bank, climbed to the top, and did it again.

(Oliver admires himself and whistles loudly.)

Reader: You ask, "What good could this do? If it is so much fun, how could it be so good?"

(All the animals are doing their own thing. Oliver Otter throws water in the air.)

Reader: That's easy. Each of us has something to contribute. With every splash and every swim, Oliver threw water in the air. In the air the water grabbed some precious oxygen. Oliver's splashing and swimming mixed it around through the pond.

(Oliver Otter comes up with worms and grass in mouth.)

Reader: With every dive, Oliver brought some more worms and grass bits and seeds into the water for food.

(Fonda Fish and Carol Crawdad crowd around Oliver Otter to get some worms and air.)

Reader: Then Fonda Fish and Carol Crawdad could take the oxygen and food from the water for their own bodies.

(Freddy Frog grimaces and shakes his head.)

Reader: And oh how Freddy Frog grumped about Oliver Otter. Freddy did not like Oliver's splashing and swimming about!

Freddy Frog: *(croaks loudly)* Ribbitt! Ribbitt! *(uses his tongue to catch bugs)*

Reader: Freddy knew that he owed his life to Oliver. Whenever Oliver made a big racket, swarms of insects rose above the pond. Then Freddy Frog could just gorge himself on the mosquitoes and the gnats. He nearly tied his own tongue in knots catching all the little bugs to eat.

(Freddy Frog pats his tummy.)

Reader: Then Freddy Frog sat back on a lily pad, stuffed full. He just sang to the heavens about himself.

Freddy Frog: *(croaks again, loudly)* Ribbitt! Ribbitt!

(Carol Crawdad smiles demurely.)

Reader: The quiet one was Carol Crawdad.

(Carol Crawdad smiles again.)

Reader: Lots of other animals think Carol is not very pretty. She works hard and is very kind. Everyone likes her.

(Carol Crawdad busies herself building a nest. It could be sticks, a blanket of moss, or whatever she could use as a home.)

Reader: Carol moved around the pond gathering bits of rock and moss and twigs. Then Carol made a nest for herself on the face of the dam with the rocks and moss and twigs. To make her nest, Carol put these materials against the face of the dam in a way that stopped the dam from leaking. If no one took care of the dam, all the water would leak out and all the animals would die.

(Fonda Fish wiggles tail.)

Reader: Especially Fonda Fish. Oh, poor, poor Fonda!

(Fonda Fish checks everything.)

Reader: Fonda Fish was very happy for the work of all the animals. She tried to help where she could. Fonda Fish swam all over the pond, inspecting the bottom of the pond and the sides of the dam to see that everything was all right.

(Fonda Fish glares at Oliver Otter.)

Reader: Sometimes she had problems with Oliver Otter. His antics sometimes brought a pile of mud into the pond and made it very hard for Fonda to see. It made her so upset. Sometimes she just wanted to bite his little ear. Oliver's clowning also brought some bits of food into the water, so Fonda Fish could not complain too much about Oliver's crazy playing. It kept her alive. Sally Skipper felt the same way about Oliver.

(Sally Skipper rearranges things. Sally Skipper arranges little nests for eggs.)

Reader: Sally Skipper spent hours trying to straighten up the surface of the pond after Oliver Otter had made a mess of it. She felt she had to push and pull every little bit of moss and soil into little rafts, then push the rafts against the side. Then she laid her eggs on these little rafts so her babies could have a nice, cozy, and homey place for a nursery. Without Oliver, Sally would have had a difficult time making nests for her eggs. She was a good housekeeper, I suppose.

(All animals get along and work together.)

Reader: Together, the animals got along well. The pond was clean, and the animals thrived. Everything was comfy and cozy. It seemed the perfect life.

(Darrell Duck sits with his head in his hands. He then rubs his tummy and moans.)

Reader: One day, not too long ago, a problem came along. Darrell Duck was not feeling well. He did not feel at all like turning tailside-up in the pond. He felt too weak to grub for feed on the bottom with his tail in the air. He felt he needed a good quack. Darrell Duck climbed out on the bank and just sat in the sun. He hoped to feel better.

(Toby Turtle checks Darrell Duck for fever.)

Reader: When Toby Turtle saw Darrell Duck out on the bank, Toby sensed trouble. Someone else would have to do some of Darrell's work or the pond would die.

(All animals wait around together and start talking to each other. They gesture wildly about a sick duck.)

Reader: Toby called the other animals to come around for a meeting. The animals all begin to talk at once about the terrible state of affairs. The panic was just about complete before Toby Turtle took over.

(Toby Turtle takes over meeting.)

Reader: Then Toby Turtle told everyone he would immediately —
or at least when he could get to it, with his busy schedule and all —
he would immediately form a committee to study the issue — whatever it was that hurt Darrell Duck so much that he could not do his
work.

*(Sally Skipper produces a newspaper from somewhere and waves
it in the air.)*

Reader: After the committee studied the issue, Toby would help
the committee design a statement. Every leader must have a statement about something before the leader could act. That must be
what a leader does — follow statements made by committees! Toby
would print the statement in a paper or read it on television, and
that would solve the problem, or something like that.

(All huddle up again.)

Reader: Television commentators seemed to often call for strong
action or at least strong words. The words would lead to serious
steps by the population.

(All animals hold their noses and gesture toward the pond.)

Reader: *(much more intense)* The pond was becoming very un-
clean now while everyone waited. And waited. Strong words would
surely clear up the situation. The pond was muddied more now by
unclear commitments. These commitments would now become
clear as Toby took charge. Clearly now, in confused times such as
these now faced by the citizens, the pond needed Toby's leadership. The pond often needed Toby's leadership. This was a difficult
time. It was always bad when such a thing might happen that a
duck gets a tummyache.

(Toby Turtle appoints others to do this and that. He points out things for them to do.)

Reader: So Toby Turtle appointed many others to make plans and write instructions for dealing with such things. He named himself to name others for the rest of the work. He must clear things up.

(Toby Turtle lays down to take a nap.)

Reader: Toby Turtle only wanted to see to it that something was done. He was not too certain about doing any of the work himself. Toby Turtle had already missed too much sleep today. So, nothing happened just then. Toby needed a nap. He pulled his head back into his shell and took a small siesta.

(Carol Crawdad wanders off very slowly.)

Reader: Carol Crawdad heard that a committee was forming, so Carol said, "I am sure the others will not need me to do any planning or talking. I do not know what to do. I must wait for someone to tell me what to do. I wouldn't want to do something now. I probably would have to change it later." Because waiting is boring, Carol went off to find some excitement. Perhaps she could watch bananas ripen or watch ice melt or watch moss grow.

(Oliver Otter stands around thinking. He hangs his head.)

Reader: Oliver Otter, hearing that Carol Crawdad had gone off searching for excitement, thought about the lack of excitement in his own life. He suddenly thought of the great life of a professional athlete. Excitement, lots of money and honor! The headlines on the sports pages always told of he wonderful things some athletes had done. The athlete could say, "I gots!" and no one would criticize.

(Oliver Otter shows off his muscles. He runs around a little. Then he sits like "The Thinker.")

Reader: Oliver quit his work. He had never thought of it as work before. He could train full-time for the Pond Olympics. He could spend his time in training for his work. This was really just playing at working. Hour after hour of running and lifting, lifting and running were now paying off. These efforts brought him to this wonderful condition. Oliver only slid down the bank into the water when someone would pay him to do it. He trained hard for the Pond Olympics. He really wasn't eligible because he acted only for money. Maybe he could cheat, just a little. Or maybe the International Pond Olympics Committee would change the rules to make him eligible.

(Sally Skipper tried to organize the animals into a legislative body.)

Reader: Sally Skipper saw all the work that needed to be done. Sally began lobbying in Pond Congress for a law to ban moss and leaky dams and unsolvable problems. Sally spent her time writing the proper law and trying to give herself a raise in pay rather than cleaning up the pond. Then she began to hold hearings on whether someone had lied when they said the pond was never dirty.

(Freddy Frog sits and rocks.)

Reader: Poor Freddy Frog. The task at hand stretched his mind and body too far. He simply crawled up on a lily pad and croaked. The pad was just like a rocking chair — back and forth, back and forth. Freddy Frog thought this really wasn't bad at all.

(Someone could throw a green blanket over Fonda Fish and others of the cast.)

Reader: Sad Fonda Fish was in real trouble. No oxygen or good food was coming into the pond. The animals weren't playing now. A green slime was spreading over the top of the pond. Fonda Fish was dying.

(Fonda Fish prepares to die.)

155

Reader: With a last gasp and a little wiggle of her tail, Fonda rose to the top of the pond. She began to roll over on her back, ready for the sad end she knew was coming. She knew the problems well. She just could not make anyone listen.

(Fonda Fish throws a little water into the air. Then some more and more. She wiggles her tail excitedly.)

Reader: She was not ready to go just yet. She would go down fighting, if she had to go. Thrashing about with her tail, Fonda Fish made a little splash. She threw some water into the air where it soaked up some air. That little splash brought a little oxygen into the water for Fonda. It gave her some new strength. She realized she could help herself that way, so she thrashed some more. Then some more.

(Oliver Otter is napping, but opens an eye and frowns when Fonda Fish splashes him. Then he gets excited.)

Reader: Oliver Otter — he wasn't too bright, really — but Oliver saw Fonda Fish making such a ruckus on the pond! He thought, "That looks like fun. Why didn't I think of having fun doing that?"

(Oliver Otter has fun splashing and diving.)

Reader: Then Oliver Otter began to swim and dive and splash in the pond. Sliding down the bank looked great! His muscles were strong and healthy from all his exercises and training. He was even able to do a little flip just before he hit the water.

(Freddy Frog has lunch of insects.)

Reader: The thrashing and smashing and diving and sliding of Oliver brought swarms of insects up out of the weeds and the moss. Freddy Frog, who was hungry by now, began to eat and eat and eat. He said, "That's a good one. I like gnats. They are quite tasty and even a little crunchy." Freddy ate until his tongue was so tired from catching insects that it felt like he had tied his tongue into a knot.

(Toby Turtle eats and eats and eats.)

Reader: Toby Turtle, watching Freddy eat, felt hungry and began to dig around with his flippers. He found tender roots and grass to eat. He even thought about stashing some food inside his shell for those times when he might be hungry again!

(Sally Skipper body-surfs on the pond.)

Reader: One of Oliver Otter's big splashes made a wave that nearly threw Sally Skipper out on the bank. She had so much fun! Sally went back for more. All the activity made lots of pieces of moss and grass come to the top of the water. Sally Skipper started gathering them for her little nests again.

(Darrell Duck pulls on a worm with his bill.)

Reader: Darrell Duck saw that the waves in the pond were washing the mud off a spaghetti bowl of fresh worms. They looked so good! He just could not resist them. He pulled on one until it came out. Then he ate it in one big gulp while he grabbed for another.

(The animals move back to their original positions, doing what comes naturally.)

Reader: All the animals together now brought the pond back to life by doing what came naturally. The community had nearly let the pond and everything in it die, but they saved it! They loved every minute of the work, but they did not think it was hard work. They thought it was fun. The pond lived on.

The Big Feed

Synopsis: The essence of being human is in being loved. It is not to love that we live, but to be loved. When God loves us, it is *Hesed* — Steadfast Love. It will neither quit nor be withdrawn.

Liturgical Calendar: Thanksgiving or Easter 5, any cycle

Scriptures: Haggai 1:1b—2:9; Psalm 145:1-5, 17-21; 2 Thessalonians 2:1-5, 13-17; Luke 20:27-38 or Acts 8:26-40; Psalm 22:25; 1 John 4:7-21; John 15:1-8

Comment: A true story.

Note: This can be a monologue with actions. Make signs for each participant. For larger groups, make multiple signs for each character. For smaller groups, give the participants more than one sign. The story lists about 55 characters. Actions should be the things that one does at a large family meal, such as talking, cooking, eating, and playing. Have fun.

Ten of us living in our little house was a bit much. Two boys, six girls, and Mom and Pop sort of crowded out even the roaches and flies in our home. We had a basement house. No upper level, just a small attic. The attic was large enough to store the Christmas decorations, and well, a couple of spiders.

The basement was sixteen feet wide by 24 feet long. The walls and floor were concrete. Part of the living area had simple rugs.

Our laundry room was outside. So was the bathroom. In the coldest weather, we took our weekly baths inside in a galvanized iron tub. It took four tubs of water, one after the other. One tub for the youngest three girls and for my brother, Roy. One for the oldest three, one for me, and one for our parents. It seems crude today.

Still, it was a good tradition.

I was usually last in the tub. Dirty kids must wait. Hallelujah! Those days of milking cows and feeding pigs, chickens, and sheep qualified me to use a tub of water all to myself. That meant I was last so I could wash off all the sweat and grime. Perhaps no one wanted to use the bathwater after me.

That was a good thing.

Meals were a big part of the Evans' family tradition. The Tish family, Mom's family, really put more emphasis on meals. We had many meals at the Tish family home, near Greanleaf, Idaho.

Before 1948, many of us gathered early at the Tish home on Thanksgiving or Christmas. When we arrived, I would go directly out into the shop. Grandpa always seemed to lay out a new tool or piece of harness in his blacksmith shop for me to look at. I always pored over the new tool and tried to understand how Grandpa made it. More importantly, I tried to understand its purpose. Often I could not. I still have one of his products that I do not understand.

Then I wandered around among the dairy cows and calves. I just liked to feel the goodness of their presence and warmth.

It was a good tradition.

Wandering around the Tish farm by myself gave me peace. Sometime in the afternoon someone would come find me. By this time, the rest of the cousins and neighbors were at Ira and Mamie's. Grandma demanded I wash up outside then come in the house. The crowd was huge and they were waiting for me. I was ready.

It was a good tradition. I could eat 'til I was full.

1948 was different. Everything had to change. We had a new house! In the summer of 1948, we built the upper level on our house. We simply lifted off the roof, using hay derricks. Then we built the walls and stood them up. We even nailed some exterior sheathing on them before we stood them in place.

We lifted the roof up and set it up on the walls, and we had our upper level. Mom was so happy! She had a regular kitchen with running water, an electric stove, an electric water heater, and built-in cupboards. She had a plan, and she had faith. Her plan would fit nicely in the family faith tradition.

To celebrate our new addition, Mom and Pop decided to have the family Thanksgiving dinner at our place. Mom set about inviting those who should come that year. They came from both sides of the family and from the neighborhood. This was such a big occasion even Grandpa and Grandma Evans came from across the road. They did not come over very often. Yet they came on that Thanksgiving. It was to become a good part of our faith tradition.

Grandpa and Grandma Evans and Aunt Janice lived just a couple hundred feet away. I went over there to work for them sometimes, but it was not always comfortable. It really did not matter. Everything I did was outdoors — milking cows, stacking hay, irrigating.

Grandpa was a ranking Democrat in Idaho then. My father was Payette County Republican chairman. One evening before an election we had a community reception for the Republican candidate for Congress at our home. Across the road, Grandpa and Grandma Evans were hosting a meet-and-greet for the Democrat.

It was a fine tradition, being patriotic and independent.

Uncle Sherman and Aunt Doris, with their children: Kenny, Carol, Kathy, Christine, and Keith were more of my family. I really enjoyed working for them in my teens. Sherman had one good eye and a quick smile. He was also a fascinating inventor. Sometimes, while we worked, we talked over an idea for some new tool. The next day, Uncle Sherman would bring out the first copy. He sometimes worked late at night or early in the morning to make the tool. Often it was still hot from the forge when he brought it out.

Uncle Sherman and I had a good tradition together.

On the day before Thanksgiving, Pop and I and Mom and Deanna went to the Grange Hall and we borrowed several long tables. These tables were just three eight-foot one-by-twelves nailed together on crosspieces. The legs were just simple sawhorses. We also borrowed lots of chairs.

I did not know who or how many were coming to dinner that day. I just sensed that it would take an act of God to get all the food

160

on the tables. Everyone needed a place to sit. We arranged the tables in a large "L" in the house.

On Thanksgiving morning, Deanna and I did chores, as usual. It took a couple of hours to milk the cows. Then we had to feed the cows and pigs and sheep and chickens and horses. By the time I came back in the house, the tables were starting to load up. They already had cloths and some decorations on them.

By the time everyone came that day, it was good that we had not had time to put up the sheet rock on the wall interiors. We had not installed insulation, yet. It gave us extra room to squeeze the smaller kids between the two-by-fours.

Mom and Pop had also invited some neighbors — Jay Williams and his wife, Mary. Jay had a team of white horses. They were beautiful together. They were gentle and patient and strong.

Jay was terribly proud of his horses. He spent much time cleaning and grooming and training them. Mary Williams was a great cook. She brought pies and garden stuff: corn and beans and tomatoes and relishes. Of course, those were just for me. It was a great tradition she and I had together. She cooked. I ate. I could feel the love.

Sam Henne came. Sam and his wife, Greta, were German Jews. They had escaped from Hitler before WWII. They purchased a small piece of land near our home. They built a small house with one bedroom and a kitchen. The Hennes worked hard to become Americans. They were proud to bring a cooked turkey to the Thanksgiving dinner. They lived the tradition — hard work, church, debt, citizenship — it was good. The tradition they had of sharing their new life with the neighbors really felt good. They did not have much, but they shared.

The Tish families came early. First came Grandpa and Grandma Tish. They came from Greenleaf about eight or nine o'clock in the morning. The Tishes would have come earlier, I believe, if they could have. However, they had to milk cows and feed chickens. Later they had lots of chickens, maybe a hundred thousand or so.

Grandma brought lots of food — cranberry sauce, a ham, sweet potatoes already cooked, pickles, jam, rolls, and pies. I can still smell the trunk of their 1947 Chevy even today. That is why I bought that car from them when they sold it. I wanted a car that smelled like Thanksgiving dinner. What could one expect from a growing boy?

Talk about fine traditions of love!

Grandpa Tish needed to feel important. Grandma always ran things in her own home. Grandpa was just around to work hard and pay for the stuff Grandma wanted.

At our home that fine Thanksgiving day, there really was nothing for Grandpa to do. I guess he mostly sat around, bored. It was traditional, but maybe not such a good tradition.

Then came Aunt Anna, Mom's sister, and her husband, Bob. Bob had some personal problems. He later fought in Korea. The family said he came home with a broken heart from the violence. Then we called it battle fatigue. Now, we call it Post-Traumatic Stress Disorder (PTSD).

Wars are not a fine tradition, but a traditional failure of the human spirit.

We tried to turn it into a tradition of love, but we were not very successful. Deanna is my next older sister. She and I sometimes talked about this while we milked the cows. I did not understand then, and I still don't. Why do we need wars?

Anyway, Bob and Anna came, and brought their children: Larry, Patty, and Beverly. They came, and that was good.

George and Mabel were at our house. Mabel was Mom's sister. She was a favorite. Mabel was a nurse, and George was a Nazarene pastor at the time. Their son, Terry, came, and their daughter, Mary Lou.

Aunt Bea and Uncle Oral came. Oral was Mom's brother. He was a real talker. One day I asked Grandpa why they spelled Oral with an "A" instead of an "E," as most spell the name. Grandpa was silent for a few moments. Off someplace, we could hear Oral telling some long-winded story to anyone who would listen. Grandpa smiled, looked at me and simply said, "Do you really need to ask?"

Laughter is a good tradition.

162

It is a real tradition built on love. It felt good to be in on the joke. Grandpa told me many jokes. We can even repeat some of them.

Such a loving tradition!

I did admire Uncle Oral. He was married to Aunt Bea. I thought she was the prettiest woman in the whole world. She was also maybe the nicest. When she smiled, even the clouds rolled away so more light could shine on her face. Her daughter, Barbara, was almost as pretty as Bea was, as was Paulette. The younger boy, Eugene, was cute — not cuddly — just cute.

The oldest son, Gary, now an insurance broker in Seattle, was trouble for me. We fought some when he did not stay in the house where he belonged. I told him.

Oral and Bea brought some good things: potatoes, a beef roast or two, plus corn and squash. Maybe they brought cookies and pies, and probably plates and water glasses.

The tradition of sharing for Thanksgiving is a good one.

Everyone had a job. It was all done for me, I was certain.

Phyllis, my oldest sister, had started chasing Arlon about that time, I guess. She eventually married him. In 1949, she was too young to invite him to come to dinner. He was only sixteen and she was fourteen. She made herself busy helping Mom. Phyllis probably spent some time thinking she could not live through the day without Arlon.

Evelyn was the studious one of the family. She was a little quieter than most of us, I believe. Whenever she could, she read. Evelyn always had a book she needed to read. She worked hard on this great day. Everyone did.

After all, it was tradition.

Deanna and I milked the cows and finished most of the other outside chores. I usually did what she said. She could whip me easily then.

Marilyn put out the plates and cups and glasses. She was eight at the time. Marilyn sometimes helped with the everyday chores. At eight she was not able to do much except feed the livestock.

163

Sally and Freda handled the eating utensils — knives, forks, and spoons. We had no napkins. No one I knew had such things. We expected to eat without getting dirty. Only city folks ate so carelessly they became dirty from the food — uncivilized.

Roy was just a year and ten months old. He probably just sat in his high chair and fussed or slept. When Roy was four or five years old, he usually had a fork in one hand and a spoon in the other while Pop prayed. When Pop said, "Amen," Roy put both tools to work immediately. He also tended to sleep during the prayer. One day he went to sleep. Then Pop said, "Amen!" Roy forgot what he was doing. He tried to grab a piece of chicken with the spoon. Then he stabbed himself in the back of that hand with the fork that was in his other hand. I guess that was Roy's own tradition.

Sometime during the morning, a woman we did not know came to the door. This visitor was about forty, I suppose. She said she was walking to Boise. That was about another fifty miles. She offered to do some work around our place in return for some food — maybe she could wash dishes or something. Mom could not think of a job just then, but Mom told her she could eat with us if she wanted.

She gladly agreed. Then she did a strange thing. The new guest went to the front window and waved, as if beckoning to someone outside. Another woman and a man and a young girl showed up. We gave them the same privileges. The new guests sat and ate with the rest of us.

Thanksgiving was a tradition of love at our house.

Corinne and Geraldine Fry came. They lived just a little ways away. The Fry-Jenkins family had many children. Feeding them was a problem. They would probably have had fried goat meat for dinner on Thanksgiving, and perhaps the girls did not want that. They were about ten and twelve years old. Teenyboppers dissatisfied with the parents' provision are also a tradition. That tradition helps when parents are trying to get the children to leave home.

The older half-sister of Corinne and Geraldine, Mary Jo, came with them. We had no "friends of the family" at our house — we just expanded to include them as family.

I like that tradition.

We started eating at about nine that morning when the first food showed up. Preparations for big dinners are always invitations to grab something. Starting early is part of Thanksgiving meal tradition. A roll. A sliver of ham. An olive. Some walnuts.

The rest of the crowd just sort of showed up. Bob and Richard Imbler, the local bachelor brothers. Mom always tried to get either of them interested in Aunt Janice. It was a fun tradition for some of us. I do not know how much fun it was for Bob or Richard or Aunt Jan.

Gene and Katie Honey came. Gene worked at the mill with Pop. Later, Gene baled hay for us. He drove John Deere equipment.

Our family tradition was Farmall, but I thought I would rather have had John Deere. They were noisier. Pop thought they were weak.

Harry and Doris Woods came early, for them. Harry owned and operated the threshing machine for most of the community. Once or twice each year, Harry came down the road with his McCormick-Deering tractor and a huge threshing machine to thresh our grain and clover seed. The tractor had a top speed of about five miles per hour. The threshing machine with its long nose and swinging tail was the dragon of Nu Acres. This was perhaps the biggest day of the year. Our crop, our land payments, and our new clothes for school were at risk. They all depended on Harry Woods bringing that dragon to our place. The dragon was a very good tradition.

Henry and Martha Orcutt were friends and they belonged to the grange. Mom and Pop were grangers, too. The Orcutts lived a few miles away, across from the Carys, but they were close neighbors.

Getting close to the folks we work with is a good tradition.

Jim and Annie Cruzen and their son, Duane, came, empty-handed. I could see that Mom was relieved. Usually, when they came to a meal, they brought the same thing. In the morning of the meal, Duane took his .22 out into the sagebrush and killed a few rabbits. Then his Annie fried them up for the community meal. My mom did not think that was very pleasant. She did not like their tradition. She especially did not like fried rabbit. Nor did I. However, it was their gift and their tradition.

Enoch and Jeanine Nye, the pastor and his wife, came. The Nyes were very old. The Nye family provided pastors for many churches in Idaho, Oregon, and Washington. I liked him a lot. He mostly just smiled and let her talk. That is a fine tradition for pastors. Could I follow it better? Probably, but perhaps I do not wish to.

The Smits came — Mr. and Mrs. Smit. I never did know their first names. Even their last name was a puzzle to me. They lived in a house that was eight feet by sixteen feet. I measured it once. Their outhouse was almost the same size as their home. I helped dig a new hole for them once. Helping those who cannot help themselves is good.

Mom's Uncle Orville, and Neva, and their son, Glenn, came from up on the hill. Like so many who were there that day, they lived in a tar-paper shack until they could put some decent siding on their home. They also put some insulation in the walls and ceiling.

Not many folks know this now, but tar-paper shacks have been a terrific American tradition. They were all right as shelter until the folks could either cover them or build something else.

Around two in the afternoon we were ready to begin eating in earnest. We had cut the turkeys and hams. The jam and butter were on the table, and the frozen corn. Potatoes filled several bowls.

Talk about fine traditions of love. All for me!

When the first course was safely on the table, the desserts magically appeared from the basement: pumpkin and mincemeat pies, Jell-O, cobbler, and cinnamon rolls.

Then we ate. Well, most of us just ate. That was another thing I could admire about Uncle Oral. Grandpa said Oral was the only man Grandpa knew who could demonstrate how long the salmon was that got away while he was eating a turkey leg and telling a joke about milking a cow, all at the same time. Oral had taught in a seminary in California a few years. Oral and Bea were part of the Friends Church tradition. That seminary was good training. He was also a fun part of the tradition of Thanksgiving, a tradition of celebrating and giving life.

Some great traditions don't last forever. Especially the tradition of waiting. We probably sat to eat at around two o'clock. We also were still at the table at three thirty.

That long meal was a great tradition.

At 3:45, Pop had to go to work. He worked at the sugar mill in Nyssa. His shift started at four o'clock that day. Just as he left, snow started to fall. Within an hour, the snow had built up three or four inches.

Finally, at about five, Deanna and I and maybe one or two cousins who did not want to help with the dishes started the evening chores. Again, we had to milk the cows. By hand, of course. Twice every day. We did not get a milking machine until the next year.

We fed the cows and bull and pigs and chickens. Marilyn and the cousins gathered the hen eggs.

Holidays are a great tradition, but the animals needed care. Animals are people too. It is a strong tradition in our world.

The Tish families, the Kecks, and all the rest helped clean up the dishes and food. Then they went home. By the time they left, we had finished the chores. The snow was about four or five inches deep, and it was getting dark.

It really was a fine tradition. We were in a miracle circumstance. We knew we were loved. We knew we loved each other. A great peace was over the land.

Paul wrote to the church at Thessalonika: "So then brothers and sisters, stand firm and hold fast to the traditions that you were taught by us, either by word of mouth or by our letter. Now may our Lord Jesus Christ himself and God our Father, who loved us and through grace gave us eternal comfort and good hope, comfort your hearts and strengthen them in every good work and word" (2 Thessalonians 2:15-17 NRSV).

www.ingramcontent.com/pod-product-compliance
Lightning Source LLC
Chambersburg PA
CBHW052005090426
42741CB00008B/1559